Praise for Dance

"*Dance* is a powerful piece of writing that will motivate readers to reanalyze the role of the neglected women of biblical times. This book will become one of the prime selections in the canon of religious literature." Zahid Sheikh, Reader's Favorite Reviewer.

"Each story reads like a captivating thriller, revealing the strength, courage, and wisdom of these unsung heroines." K.C. Finn, Award Winning Author.

Dance has received Reader's Favorite 5-star coveted review for Christian Devotion/Study.

Dance Daughters of the Most High!

Amazing Stories of Long Overlooked and Underappreciated Women in the Old Testament

Dr. Bill Senyard

Acknowledgements

I want to especially acknowledge three prominent women in my life who have each helped me see and better understand the historic struggles women have endured to be fully recognized and honored, since the earliest days of humanity. It has taken many long and hard conversations over decades for them to begin to knock down my hardened cultural walls. I want to deeply thank each of you from my heart: my daughters Aubrey Buster and Allie Senyard, and my wife and co-conspirator Eunice.

Contents

Chapter One

Introduction

"It is literally impossible to be a woman. You are so beautiful and so smart, and it kills me that you don't think you're good enough." Gloria, Barbie Movie

I f you go to the Magdala Monastery in Galilee, take some time in the chapel at the Women's Atrium. It features eight pillars, seven of which represent remarkable, some relatively unknown women who followed Jesus: Mary Magdalene (Luke 8:2), Joanna, the wife of Chuza and Susanna (Luke 8:3), Mary and her sister Martha (Luke 10:38-39), Salome, the mother of James and John, Simon Peter's mother-in-law (Matthew 8:14-15) and Mary, the wife of Clopas (John 19:25). The eighth pillar honors women of faith across all time.

Find a chair, relax, and imagine what it was like to be a Jesus follower then. These were women of unusual conviction, faith, and courage who took a lead in the important work of the Kingdom.

That is certainly not where God found these women. Living in a patriarchal society, these were women who were likely, to one degree or another, overlooked, undervalued, marginalized, and too often, voiceless.

But then God. Then God's Spirit. Then God's Gospel.

Sitting in the grand hall, I had my own "but then God" moment. I was moved by the monastery creating a space to honor women—not just the major female players like Mary—but the largely under-represented women in the New Testament, some of whom risked it all to follow Jesus. I wanted to hear their voices afresh, their stories, and more than just their names on a column. After all, these are our mothers-in-faith.

I am still wrestling with my feelings from that day. But one thing was clear, I felt charged to give these women and so many other biblical women a fresh new platform to tell their stories to a new generation.

We, women and men, should get to know these special daughters of the Most High again today. We should hear their stories. We should give them their proper due.

Yes, I am an unlikely person to tell the stories of these women saints. To expand my horizons, I have intentionally pursued the expertise of women scholars, many of whom took up this same challenge long before me. I have greatly benefited from dialoguing with them.

To add yet another layer against my deep propensity to mansplain, my two daughters, scholars, and theologians in their own right, have graciously edited *Dance*. They have been tough yet kind.

Present Refocusing

Let's begin in the present. *Barbie*, the movie, splashed upon the world's scene in 2023. A summer blockbuster movie eclipsing all projections. Pink Fever and its cotton-candy-colored fantasy world arrived and landed a beachhead on the exposed shores of the "real world." The movie grossed $630 million domestically and close to $1.4 billion worldwide. It earned $337 million in revenues on its opening weekend, $155 million in the US alone. It provided sugary comfort food for anyone raised with Barbie and Ken dolls.

It became Warner Bros.'s highest-grossing domestic release of all time, surpassing the 2008 film, *The Dark Knight* and the final *Harry Potter* film. It blew away the year's other blockbusters, *Guardians of the Galaxy, Vol. 3*, *Spider-Man: Across the Spider-Verse*, and *The Super Mario Bros. Movie*.

Only fifty films in history have broken the one-billion-dollar milestone (adjusted for inflation). *Barbie* did it in three weeks. Only fourteen other films have reached the $600 million mark domestically. Director Greta Gerwig became the highest-grossing woman movie director in history.

Does it have cultural coattails? Could very well be. *Barbie* touched on an impressive number of real-life issues from the female perspective, such as motherhood, aging, women's roles, feminine identity, and sexuality."

As I sat in the theater, surrounded by a largely feminine wave of pink foam—girls, young women, older women, and some men—I witnessed something very special. Don't get me wrong, *Barbie* is a fun movie loaded with subtle humor, double entendre, and sarcasm. As *The View* host, Whoopie Goldberg proclaimed, "It's just a movie about a doll!" I originally thought so too. But it has become so much more.

The *Barbie* movie ignited new dialogue about our world. Not in some narrow, polarizing manner. It poked fun at most institutions and philosophies around today and did it in an endearing and humorous way. It turns out none of us are "Kenough."

The movie has a single moment where the audience never fails to light up. It was a surprisingly simple monologue given by Gloria, a frustrated mom, and mid-level, overlooked, and underappreciated administrator of Mattel played by America Ferrera. Those few poignant words of Gloria in the *Barbie* movie did something surprising. They brilliantly gave voice to so many women—not just here in the States, but all over the world. She spoke about the cognitive dissonance of so many women's lives in a way that made sense and was embraceable by both men and women.

> *"It is literally impossible to be a woman. You are so beautiful and so smart, and it kills me that you don't think you're good enough. Like, we have to always be extraordinary, but somehow, we're always doing it wrong. You have to be thin, but not too thin. And you can never say you want to be thin. You have to say you want to be healthy, but also you have to be thin. You have to have money, but you can't ask for money because that's crass. You have to be a boss, but you can't be mean. You have to lead, but you can't squash other people's ideas..."* Gloria, Barbie.

When I heard Gloria's monologue, I felt those very same Magdala Monastery emotions again. I wondered if Gloria speaks for those biblical women too, even across multiple millennia.

Progressive female and male scholars rightly opine that so often women's stories in the Bible have been dismissed by mainly male storytellers. In many cases, women have been stripped of their rightful place in biblical tradition, their stories told from the narrow scope of male perspectives. Their voices are sometimes silenced or overlooked.

This makes the stories of these particular Old Testament women even more remarkable. They seem to be far more spiritually aware of the presence of God, courageous and heroic, often far more than their male contemporaries—more decisive, more *righteous*—they regularly seem to care for others over themselves and often become respected authorities.

These amazing daughters of the Most High, and many others like them, were instrumental in carrying out the redemptive movement of God to the largely male-dominated world. Despite the heavily patriarchal nature of their society, these women demonstrated incredible strength, intelligence, grace, and courage. Their contributions should not be overlooked or forgotten. We are invited to learn from their stories again.

I have chosen **not** to focus on well-known female figures such as Ruth, Esther, Hagar, Miriam, the Matriarchs, Sarah, Rebekah, and others. In the *Dance*, we are going to study seven amazing, relatively unknown daughters of the Most High. Apart from the first woman we will consider, the others lived in similar patriarchal societies. Each of them had to deal with societal norms and traditions, often denying them an equal shot at value and worth—and yet, inspired by God, adored by God, and empowered by God, they each did something world-changing.

By examining the stories of these seven faithful and largely overlooked women, we can gain a deeper understanding of the significant role women have played in God's plan throughout history. As importantly, we get a more full-orbed view of the heart of God, which fiercely loves men and women equally.

In chapter three, we meet the unnamed mother of Samson. We are told she is barren, which in the culture of Israel, particularly during the time of the Judges, when "everyone did what was right in their own eyes," meant she was quite devalued. I imagine she felt helpless and broken and maybe even thought it was her fault somehow.

Certainly, she experienced her nasty, critical inner voice then too. In her book "*Yes, Please*"[1] comedian Amy Poehler described this inner enemy as "a demon voice." She writes, "This very patient and determined demon shows up in your bedroom one day and refuses to leave. You are six, or twelve, or fifteen and you look in the mirror and you hear a voice so awful and mean it takes your breath away. It says you are fat and ugly, and you don't deserve love. And the scary part is the demon is your own voice."

For this poor unnamed woman, I imagine the shaming voice said something like, "Oh barren one, you have no life to give a child. Don't look to God. This is all on you."

Yet her situation did not seem to bother God at all. God dispatched a special ambassador to speak directly to her as if she were a person of great honor and worth. I imagine this very special audience, at a time when God was largely silent, would have been both wonderful and frightening to this likely overlooked woman. So, what would empower her to risk doing what God tells her? The costs are quite high.

In chapter four, we will meet Hannah, the mother of the great prophet and king-maker Samuel. When God finds her, she is in despair. We know the source of her grief. Like the unnamed mother of Samson, she too is barren. To make matters worse, her husband's second wife, whose name can be translated as "Beautiful Flowing Hair" (you get the idea, right?) has had a child and relentlessly bullies poor Hannah. When God finds Hannah, she is riddled with societal shame and unfair social stigma. She feels unfavored. Then something happens and everything changes.

In chapter five, we meet Ya'el. Your Bible translation will probably anglicize her name, "Jael." A better transliteration of her name would be Ya'el. She is not an Israelite by birth, not an "innie." She was minding her own business when God called her up from the minor leagues to pitch in the Game—at great risk to her and her entire tribe. This was certainly nothing she was looking for or for which she felt prepared. One morning, while she was alone, the ruthless enemy general who had savagely oppressed Israel for forty years 'happened' to stumble into her compound, her home. Can you imagine? What will she do? Nothing in her upbringing came close to equipping her for such a complex situation. Where will she get the wisdom to overcome this enemy? I will tell you this. A Gentile became the template of a wise mother for the Israelites. God can do that.

Have you heard the story of how God was about to kill Moses' firstborn son? Not even an Israelite, Zipporah, had the spiritual wherewithal to read the room when Moses seemed oblivious. In chapter six, we will hear her story. Acting decisively, she stood up to God Himself.

In chapter seven, we see the enigmatic, unnamed wise woman from Abel-Beth-Maacha who, all by herself and, I believe, with remarkable God-sourced wisdom at just the right time, saves her entire city from imminent destruction.

Lastly, there is the little-known Princess Jehosheba in chapter eight, whose biblical story sounds more like a Netflix adventure thriller. At great risk to herself, in the face of horrible odds and great evil, this model of biblical righteousness rose tall. She had to. There was no one else. What she did reverberated for the next thousand years, all the way to the doorstep of a young, betrothed maiden in Nazareth.

These are some of the often-neglected stories of great women who stood up when called by God. Their stories are worthy of being included in the hallowed hall historically dominated by men. These women have every right to be called "co-redeemers of Israel and the church."

Here's a quick overview. Of these seven very special women, three weren't even Israelites (Eve, Zipporah, and Ya'el).

Except for Eve, Hannah, and the unnamed mother of Samson, the others received minuscule coverage:

The entire account of the wise woman from Abel-Beth-Maacha is laid out concisely in eight verses (2 Sam 20:15-22).

Jehosheba is mentioned in only two verses (2 Ki 11:2-3).

When God finds them:

- Three had husbands who were abusive, absent, dismissive, non-inclusive, or ineffective (Ya'el, Zipporah, and the unnamed mother of Samson). One had a perfect husband until he wasn't (Eve).

- Two were barren (Hannah and Zlelponi).

- One was named Grace. Two are unnamed. One is named "Life." Another "Yahweh is Happiness," another "Shadows." One was "Flighty Bird."

- Two (the unnamed mother of Samson and the wise woman of Abel-Beth-Maacha) are listed by Jewish midrashim[2] on the list of the twenty-three truly upright and righteous women who came out of Israel.

- Two defeated generals (Ya'el and the wise woman of Abel-Beth-Maacha).

- One overcame a ruler (Jehosheba).

- One stood up to God Himself (Zipporah).

- Three saved lives. One saved her son (Zipporah). One saved a king (Jehosheba) and one rescued an entire city (Wise Woman of Abel-Beth-Maacha).

All of them shine in contrast to the other actors on their particular stage, in particular the men.

The point? If God can do this with these unlikely regular women, most of whom were just living their normal lives when God chose them for some remarkable service, certainly God still does today.

In chapter two, we will do a deep dive into the most ideal biblical woman who has ever lived, even though we all too often forget that part of her story.

The Role of God's Spirit

These amazing daughters of the Most High were each called to do something beyond their normal capacity and experience. Were they just remarkable women who pulled it off when put in an impossible situation? Or can we see in their stories the fingerprints of God's Spirit recognizable in our lives today?

In the Old Testament period, the work of God's Spirit was not always as obvious as in the New Testament period. Paul tells us believers, God's Spirit presently dwells in our inner being (Eph 3:14-21). It is largely agreed that pre-Cross, the Spirit of God intermittently came upon regular people for specific purposes, such as to empower them with remarkable strength or wisdom to vanquish more powerful enemies, to make them willing to sacrifice their own well-being for the sake of others, to cause them to be aware of God's presence, or even to give birth to a child who has some important role in God's kingdom purposes.

If we look closely, I believe we can discern the fingerprints of God's Spirit upon these wonderful women.

- A radical sensitivity to God and His calling

- A miraculous present experience of the favor of God

- A super-human dependence upon God

- God-sourced sacrificial righteousness

- God-sourced wisdom and shrewdness

I will say more about each in the following chapters. I am often asked how modern women and men can begin to access more God-sourced capabilities and fruit. To help, we designed a very simple tool for women and men. We call it the *Simple Uncluttered Gospel*. It is not a prayer or a collection of verses per se. Think of it as a gospel presentation for the unreached people group in your brain, your critical inner voice.

That nasty voice in your head might be telling you, you have already messed up too much. Sure, God can love Billy Graham, Mother Theresa, Beth Moore, or Pope John Paul II, but God has little patience with you anymore.

So, we designed the *Simple Uncluttered Gospel*[3] to challenge the deeply rooted destructive critical inner voice. Here it is. Just sit back and let it wash over you.

Jesus-Follower, strictly because of what Jesus did for you 2000 years ago, Jesus loves you with all His heart, as much as the Father loves the Son and the Son loves the Father. God loves you as you are, not as you should be or could be. You can't add to this love or take away from it. It often feels like you've messed it up or need to do something so God will like you better. Not so. How do you experience it more? Simple! Ask the Spirit inside of you to make you know, experience and feel just how much God loves you right now. Just ask. Ask again later today. Ask tomorrow. Make it a spiritual habit.

There is neuroscience involved. We recommend you say the *Simple Uncluttered Gospel* twice a day, word for word, for 45 days. We are trying to create a new habit to compete with the nasty inner voice. Take notes on how the *Simple Uncluttered Gospel* hits you, what leaps off the page, what you haven't heard before or recently, or even what you disagree with.

Welcome to the dance, daughters of the Most High.

---

1. Poehler, *Yes Please*, 15.

2. Midrash is ancient Jewish Biblical interpretation and exegesis prominent in the Talmud and other rabbinic literature compiled between 200 and 1000 CE. "Midrash is an interpretive act, seeking the answers to religious questions (both practical and theological) by plumbing the meaning of the words of the Torah. Midrash responds to contemporary problems and crafts new stories, making connections between new Jewish realities and the unchanging biblical text." My Jewish Learning, "What is Midrash?" lines 1-8.

3. Simple Uncluttered Gospel bookmarks are available at https://gospel-app.com/product/women-simple-uncluttered-gospel-bookmarks/.

Chapter Two

Eve: The Ideal Biblical Woman

H istory has often treated Eve unfairly. Here is a legitimate complaint from a feminist theologian.

"The story of Eve in the book of Genesis has had a more profoundly negative impact on women throughout history than any other biblical story...Early Christian writers depicted Eve as subordinate and inferior to Adam—because she was created after and from him—and as weak, seductive, and evil, the cause of Adam's disobedience."[1]

Let me say on behalf of so many theologians, biblical scholars, commentators, and church leaders—mostly men—"Guilty as charged." We can't be proud of it, nor can we just say a collective, "Our bad!" and think we all enter a group hug. Meaningful reparation of trust will be slow and will require ongoing miracles of healing from the very hands of God.

Let me be clear, I am not going to pile on Eve. She is the only woman, on this side of heaven, who could stake a claim to being the most perfectly whole woman ever. She was the ideal biblical woman until she wasn't.

My belief is if Eve hadn't been the first one to grab a bit of the forbidden fruit, Adam would have eventually gotten around to it, likely late at night, hungry, wondering what might taste good, and *boom*, the serpent would have been right at his side.

I imagine the results would have been the same, likely the curses would have been similar as well. After all, Adam and Eve were cut out of the same cloth—literally. I am pretty sure Adam would have offered the fruit to Eve, and she likely would have taken it. Different story, same result.

I also believe we will see both in Heaven, both fully restored to God and each other, both filled with joy. Ideal humanity, woman, and man. Like you and me, Jesus had to die for their sins as well. Their shortcomings are no worse or better than my own.

They were the first in order, not degree, to look for significance, security, and belonging somewhere other than God's embrace, rather than God's positive measuring gaze. Eve and Adam were the first to know shame, guilt, and fear. They were the first to be hurt by relationships. They were the first to hurt others relationally. They were the first to know isolation and loneliness. But certainly not the last.

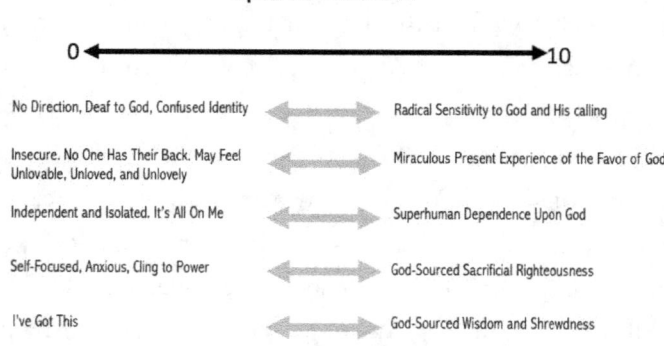

I mentioned in the introduction if we looked carefully, we could begin to observe five distinct fruit of the Spirit of God evident in the lives of these remarkable women.

- A radical sensitivity to God and His calling

- A miraculous present experience of the favor of God

- A super-human dependence upon God

- God-sourced sacrificial righteousness

- God-sourced wisdom and shrewdness

Eve and Adam, empowered by the Spirit, experienced all five, at least until the Fall, until the Spirit was removed from them. Let's consider each of these fruit separately.

Radical Sensitivity to God and His Calling

Empowered with this fruit of the Spirit, women and men seem to hear God's voice when no one else does—a little or a lot. They seem to know what God wants them to do and are empowered with a wonderful and frightening compulsion to obey, even at great risk.

Let's briefly review the Genesis story.

> *Then God said, "Let us make man (i.e., man and woman) in our image, in our likeness, and let them rule over the fish of the sea and the birds of the air, over the livestock, over all the earth, and over all the creatures that move along the ground." So, God created man in his own image, in the image of God he created him; male and female he created them. God blessed them and said to them, "Be fruitful and increase in number; fill the earth and subdue it." (Gen 1:26-28)*

One of the most identifiable fingerprints of the person whom the Holy Spirit empowers, male or female, is they seem to hear God's voice a little clearer than others and seem to be a little more aware of God's presence, calling, and purpose. To one degree or another, they have better answers to the important questions, "Who am I?" and "Why am I here?" Eve and Adam were the only humans ever who truly understood who they were with God and each other and why they were created—until they didn't. I am going to refer to this as *relational actualization.*

The concept of "self-actualization" is looming large in the West today. Self-actualization comes from Maslow's hierarchy of needs, which you probably studied at one time or another. Self-actualization is the highest level of psychological development, where a person realizes their own potential only after their security, ego, and bodily needs have been fulfilled. Some see the recent *Barbie* movie as the main character's journey to finding herself—to being actualized.[2]

With apologies to Maslow, Eve and Adam went far beyond self-actualization, which can end up being very me-oriented and isolating. They found actualization and wholeness in their relationship with God and each other. They knew *Immanuel*, God with us.

When you see them in your mind, don't imagine two *independent,* isolated people. In Genesis 1, it is impossible to speak of Adam's role apart from Eve, or Eve's apart from Adam. They were uniquely God's reflection, male and female, without any priorities, subjugation, or caveats. Adam and Eve were God's reflection—together—clear distinctions, but no substantive inequalities or subservience.

Can you imagine how they might have felt? You have probably asked at one time or another what God's will was for your life. Adam and Eve knew.

They were both equally charged with the overarching godlike goal of being fruitful, multiplying, filling, ruling, and subduing. For simplicity's sake, I will use the acronym BFMFRS.

How were Adam and Eve related?

"The Lord God said, 'It is not good for the man to be alone. I will make a helper ('ezer) suitable for him'"(Gen 2:7-18).

Helper (Hebrew: *'ezer*) has two main meanings. *'Ezer* often speaks of military assistance required by treaties and covenants. If a country is under siege, they look to their covenant partners to send an army to save them—to be an *'ezer* in a battle that is overwhelming.

The second connotation is a person who helps the hurting, the needy. I am not aware of any passage where the connotation is a lower-level assistant. The Psalmists often refer to God as their *'Ezer.*

"Hear, O LORD, and be merciful to me; O LORD, be my help ('ezer)" (*Psalm 30:10*).

"Surely God is my help ('ezer); the Lord is the one who sustains me" (Psalm 54:4).

Would it change things for us to see Eve as strategically needed because of all the trouble humanity, and particularly the sons of Adam, were going to get into in their attempt to accomplish all the messy subduing, ruling, filling, and multiplying? Let's face it. Adam would have a really hard time trying to accomplish the "filling and multiplying" thing without Eve. Adam could shape dirt and blow on it all he wants—it's just not going to happen.

It is equally true about ruling and subduing. What needed to be subdued and ruled in a perfect creation? Of course, Satan! Adam and Eve were ordered to subdue and rule over the much stronger foe, Satan. If they had pulled it off, I imagine the angels would have been as surprised as anyone. If the first couple had done it, the sixty-six books would just be a mini-series![3]

From the beginning, Eve was a necessary, equally honored participant and co-lead in the plan for humanity's glory alongside Adam, and both were equally dependent upon God. There would be no BFMFRS without her. Eve was never secondary in status. Eve was not made from the ground like Adam but was specifically pulled from his substance, "out of" his essence. It is biblically absurd to argue that women are of a lesser substance than men. They were both of the very same stuff (Gen 2:21-23).

Effectual Assurance of God's Favor and Love

Eve and Adam were also the only humans ever who really *fully* experienced God's favor—

...until they didn't.

I imagine Pre-Fall Eden as a place where woman and man equally experienced an ongoing sense of God's favor and love for each as they were, not as they should be or could be. This is so important. It is how we were created.

Child psychologist Urie Bronfenbrenner said something so insightful and on point here. "Every child needs at least one adult who is irrationally crazy about him or her."[4] Isn't that right? We are all jonesing for at least one person who sees us that way.[5]

We saw it in the Garden, I believe. Eve experienced such *favor* perfectly until she didn't. Adam too.

Superhuman Dependence Upon God

Adam and Eve were the only humans to ever live fully dependent upon God—until they didn't.

We really must dig deep to imagine this one. The plan was to BFMFRS, not on our own, but dynamically *dependent* upon God's capacity.

Let's look at biblical dependence. Today, "dependence" is a four-letter word. It has come to have negative connotations and reflect a power imbalance, often male-dominated, that can hurt, dehumanize, and shame. I imagine a hard weaponized Louisville Slugger bat with the words "submit" and "obey" burned into the barrel.

Biblical dependence is very different. Let me characterize this "dependence" as an intentional and free reliance upon the capacity of another who deeply cares for you and is willing to die to honor you. It gives up illusions of control and carries no negative element of subordination or subjugation. It has no connotation of being right or wrong, or doing right or not doing wrong. No grades, no judgment, no shaming, no weakness. It is a choice made by a free agent. To accomplish the high tasks we are given, we will need far more than our own capabilities.

Let me offer a metaphor that might be helpful. Consider the mutual dependence of skilled dancers. Next time you're on a dance floor and couples come together, arm in arm in sync with the music, take a moment to look around. All the couples are relatively together and more or less in rhythm.

Yet find that one couple who have remarkably captured the rhythm, or better, are captured by it. One partner leads the dance, but not to the detriment of the other. The other is not rigidly being forced to follow against their will but is willingly being swept up into the movement of mutual dance. Both are sensitive to the mind, spirit, and capability of the other. There is not a differentiation of relative power or subjugation in any way, but rather a mutual syncopation, an in-sync-ness, a oneness, where both are accomplishing a single goal that individually would look quite silly. There is mutual joy, equality, and no sense of compulsion, or insecurities about the left foot or right foot next. No one gets more credit. No one gets less.

In my younger years, I had a reputation as being quite a dancer. Don't get me wrong, it wasn't so much that people stood back in awe as they watched me dance. God forbid. But I did come in second in a disco contest once. I digress.

As a reasonably skilled dancer, my partners trusted that in my arms they would have a good experience. They wouldn't look foolish, or feel like they were being graded, or used. They were able to relax, get into the movement, and enjoy the experience of the dance, along with me.

It turns out humans were created by God for such dependence. It begins in infancy with *attunement*. Dr. David E. Arredondo explains the power of caregiver-infant attunement during the first year of life. Imagine a mother holding her infant and intentionally gazing into his or her eyes.

> "This mother and this baby are in a process...a form of reciprocal connectedness called attunement. His eyes and her eyes are locked together—not locked together—but dancing together, really. And in this child's brain, a thousand connections per second are being formed, and this child is learning to read facial expression. This child is learning about the world. He's learning that the world is responsive or not responsive. He's learning that he can be an object of delight and that he can delight others; he's learning what he's worth. He's learning what the world is like. He's learning so much so quickly that we can't even conceive of it."[6]

Humans are one of the few mammals born totally dependent on their caregivers. Not just for food and security, but for emotional well-being.[7]

It's brain science. I submit we are equally wired to experience a similar ongoing dependence on God where we actively begin to feel understood by

God more and more. Otherwise, we will tend to spiritually dysregulate and fall into the "everyone did right in their own eyes cycle." No judgment; we all do it.

Have you heard this? Adam and Eve had that kind of life-changing daily relationship with God until they didn't. I sometimes try to imagine how they felt day-to-day.

Recently, I was playing peek-a-boo with a young child on a plane. Often, people don't want to sit in the same row as an infant. I don't mind at all. She was a happy child, maybe 10 months old. I looked at her and smiled. She looked at me and smiled back. I looked away for a second and then looked back at her. She was still locked in. I smiled again; she smiled back. I did this two or three more times. The young girl started to laugh and move her arms excitedly up and down. Her parents loved the positive attention she was getting. Though her undeveloped infant brain couldn't make any sense of what she was feeling or what the rules of the game were all about, she was smiling and laughing, clearly having a good time. At that moment, there were no obvious anxieties about flying. No worries about getting it right. No worries about whether she was attractive or lovable enough. No concern for what others thought of her. Even though she didn't have the words, she likely felt honored, noticed, appreciated, or, in a word, liked. She had no obvious insecurities that made her hide her face in her parents' arms.

Adam and Eve likely felt the very same seminal feelings drenched 24/7 in God's adoring, measuring gaze. There is a common metaphor in Hebrew, *lipnay Elohim* or *lipnay Yahweh*. Literally, one could translate it crudely, as "in front of God's nose" or "up in God's grill." Most often, the phrase is translated boringly as "in the presence of God," but it is so much more than that. It refers to those moments when, by faith, you are gazing up into God's eyes and seeing just how much God adores you, is proud of you, is so excited you are looking up, and you feel so special—just like an infant gazing up at the eyes of his or her adoring mother.[8]

Is this human need for ongoing dynamic *lipnay Elohim* a new concept for you? Adam and Eve only knew a deluge of *lipnay Elohim* toward them. I believe they would have never felt its absence. That may have been part of the problem. That's _all_ they knew. Nowhere is it written before the Fall that they were warned to stay up in God's face or walk in the light of God's measuring gaze.

No one ever told me about gravity. Gravity just is. I learned about gravity the hard way, just like everyone else. I fell. It took me a while, but I figured it out. Adam and Eve found out the hard way too. That's all they knew until they didn't. It took a fall, I suppose. No judgment. I would have done the very same thing. In fact, I do it daily. The 5th-century influential theologian Augustine concluded unless a man or woman regularly,

> "turns towards the immutable good which is God, and stands firm in him, he cannot be formed so as to be just and happy...Man is not so constituted that he would be able, when once created, to perform any good deed by his own powers . . . All his good action consists in his being turned to Him by whom he has been made, and in his becoming, by his creator's power, just, faithful, wise, and blessed always."[9]

With apologies, I am going to abscond and revise author and Clinical Professor of Psychiatry Dr. Dan Siegel's words related to mother/infant attunement and apply them to an attuning connection with God [alterations noted].

> "When we attune with [God] we allow our own internal state to shift, to come to resonate with [God's] inner world ... This resonance is at the heart of the important sense of "feeling felt" that emerges in close relationships. [We] need attunement to feel secure and to develop well, and throughout our lives we need attunement to feel close and connected."[10]

I love the comment from Dr. Marks-Tarlow referring to the importance of sufficient attuning between the infant and primary caregiver. "The individual is seen to emerge out of a relationship with significant other."[11]

Eve and Adam were meant to emerge out of God's positive, adoring, measuring gaze. They would have been the only humans who ever felt secure, safe, loved, desired, appreciated, enough, and happy. Perhaps no words were exchanged, and yet they still felt, "You are My beloved son or daughter with whom I am well pleased." It was unthinkable the first two humans would ever say, "Forget it. I don't need God anymore. I've got this."

What could go wrong?

How powerful was the spiritual and relational air they breathed? Imagine yourself after a very bad day, week, or decade. You feel ashamed of who you have become, or maybe something you've done or didn't do, or what was done to you that you couldn't or didn't stop. You feel like you've messed up your life. You might feel unattractive, unlovable, or maybe even stupid. Maybe someone has abandoned you, broken up with you, divorced you. Maybe you are afraid of some dirty little secret getting out. Maybe you are like the 58% of teenage girls[12]who are feeling severely hopeless and sad. Or the 10% who have attempted suicide. Maybe you are cutting? Maybe sexting?

Stay with me here. If we could magically transport you back to the Garden, at that time and that place, how would that change the way you feel?

The fact you are in *the* garden might be a bit of a shocker, maybe even uncomfortable. You would likely have some fears others might see what you've been working hard to cover up—some physical not-enoughness.

But you notice the man, Adam is his name, shows no sign of judging, being critical, or being put off by your flaws. He seems to really like and enjoy you. There is no standoffishness at all, none you can see. In his eyes, you are more than enough. He likes what he sees. He adores you. It is only awkward for you.

But what happens next really blows you away. You look over your shoulder and you see God (just go with me here). You happen to look up into God's all-seeing and all-knowing eyes, and you know nothing is ever going to be the same. Your reflection in God's eyes is so wonderful it is troubling. You learned the hard way if it is too good to believe, it...well you know. Your midbrain's protective mechanisms kick in big time. You want to look away, but there is some alien magnetic power in God's gaze—no, in the love that pours from God's stare. You can see, that even if it is too good for your cautious, paranoid brain to compute, God adores you. There is no probation, no criticism, no hesitancy. There is no sense God is about to lecture you about the mess you've made and say, "OK, I'll give you a short leash, but don't screw it up next time! Three strikes and you're out." God is smiling at you and laughing. God speaks. God is so skilled at revelation He tells you just how spectacular you are and then jokes, after all, "I made you that way." God personally picked your eye color, your hair color, your skin color, your personality, and your stubbornness. God looks at you like a master artist gazes upon a finished masterpiece.

"You are my beloved daughter, with whom I am well pleased."

So how does that make you feel? I suspect with the years or decades of hurt, wounds, and even trauma from so many relationships gone south, your midbrain is still pushing back. But hopefully, it is losing its power a little. Maybe it has met its match—a greater power, the power of God's love. Something is also happening in your soul. You are feeling differently about yourself. You may be feeling a little more attractive, lovable, hopeful, or maybe even happier—more the woman you were meant to be. You are feeling a little more enough. You may even feel hope. You might just be getting an urge to dance—a little.

I am suggesting this is how God made you and me. God made us dependent upon that stunning measuring gaze. The heavenly *lipnay Elohim*. Adam and Eve were never created to be independent. Neither are we.[13]

This is how it was back then, in the Garden, before all hell broke loose. Adam and Eve's sense of worth and value had always been a function of experiencing and depending upon God's celestial gaze.

Until it wasn't.

God-Sourced Sacrificial Righteousness

Eve and Adam would have been willing to die for each other—until they weren't.

Modern Christians typically understand only one narrow aspect of biblical *righteousness*. Righteousness, we say, is about *doing right* and *obeying the law*.

*"Blessed is the man who does not walk in the counsel of the
wicked or stand in the way of sinners or sit in the seat of mockers.
But his delight is in the law of the LORD, and on his law, he
meditates day and night" (Ps 1:1-3).*

Blessed is the woman, or man, who does the right thing. Amen.

While righteousness includes "doing" right, it is vastly larger than that.
It is better to understand that "doing right" and "obeying the law" are the
necessary <u>fruit</u> of an inner God-sourced righteousness.

Let me explain. At its core, righteousness (Hebrew: *tsaddiq*) is a relational
word. It is the fulfillment of the demands of a relationship. When you are
right with someone, you express it by doing right to them. Make sense?

The woman who loves God with all her heart, mind, and soul and her
neighbor likewise is a righteous woman because, out of that God-sourced
inner love, she will "do" right things for her neighbors and God. The "root"
is love for her neighbor. The necessary "fruit" of love is loving actions toward
them. The wicked love only themselves, and their actions reflect that.

This righteousness is at the very core of Jesus' DNA. He was not acting
out of selfish motives, seeking to further himself or his reputation and
power. He acted on behalf of vulnerable others, the needy, the helpless, the
shamed. Here's Paul,

*"Do nothing out of selfish ambition or vain conceit, but in
humility consider others better than yourselves. Each of you
should look not only to your own interests, but also to the
interests of others. Your attitude should be the same as that of
Christ Jesus: Who, being in very nature God, did not consider
equality with God something to be grasped, but made himself
nothing, taking the very nature of a servant, being made in
human likeness. And being found in appearance as a man, he
humbled himself and became obedient to death-- even death on
a cross!" (Phil 2:1-11)*[14]

In his first sermon at a synagogue in His hometown, Nazareth, Jesus proclaimed,

> *"The Spirit of the Lord is on me, because he has anointed me to preach good news to the poor. He has sent me to proclaim freedom for the prisoners and recovery of sight for the blind, to release the oppressed, to proclaim the year of the Lord's favor"* *(Luke 4:18-19).*

These are words the Jewish people would have expected a "righteous king" to say upon his or her ordination to the throne. The righteous king, "is one who brings a good and happy life for all his subjects. One featured means is through edicts at the time of accession, which include the remission of debts, the freeing of slaves, and the release of the land. Thus, there is a close association with ideas of 'generosity', 'mercy' and setting free."[15]

When I look at the actions of the six daughters of the Most High in this book, I look for signs of such spiritual righteousness. Are they willing to sacrifice their safety and well-being to save others? Unfortunately, today our concept of righteousness has often devolved into a rigid adherence to the letter of the law, devoid of compassion or empathy for other people, something to be ginned up by our strength—without the need of the Spirit of God. Righteousness "describes a person rightly related to God and concerned for the well-being of others."[16]

To be clear, this righteousness is solely God-sourced, not of human making. Before the Fall, I am sure both Eve and Adam would have been willing to die for each other. But then it all went wrong.

God-Sourced Wisdom and Shrewdness

Lastly, Eve and Adam had access to all the God-sourced wisdom they could ever want—until they didn't.

Here, I am going to have to read between the lines. We know more of the personification imagery surrounding Lady Wisdom Post-Fall in Proverbs. I am going to assume God-sourced wisdom was at least equally available in the

Garden for Adam and Eve. In Proverbs, we see her roaming through the streets of the town openly urging fools to hear her words and lean on her.

> *"Wisdom calls aloud in the street, she raises her voice in the public squares; at the head of the noisy streets, she cries out, in the gateways of the city she makes her speech: 'How long will you simple ones love your simple ways? How long will mockers delight in mockery and fools hate knowledge?'" (Prov 1:20-22)*

Wisdom is presented as begotten by God in primordial time, distinct, and finite. "She preaches and pleads with a prophet's passion, thinks, and circulates with 'intellectuals' and wields the authority of God." [17]

I suggest the wisdom of God was always available to Eve and Adam. Perhaps she was screaming in Eve's ear about the dangers of the enigmatic fruit? Or the threat of the Serpent.

Better, I think all Eve had to do was turn and look into God's face and directly ask God what she should do.

But this time, she did not.

"Now the serpent was more crafty than any of the wild animals the LORD God had made" (Gen 3:1-4).

Without the specific wisdom that is God-born, Eve and Adam were forced to rely on their own wiles—no match for the 'higher knowledge'–and the lies of the Serpent, to be sure.

What Happened?

I don't imagine Satan was doing some brilliant Jedi mind trip here. I don't think this is the most subtle, sophisticated con job ever. I think it was ridiculously easy. It would have been so for Adam and for you and me as well. Satan's success then, and most often today, wasn't just to get them to eat some forbidden fruit. It was not about trying to get them or us to break this or that law. It is worse. He got them subtly thinking they could BFMFRS on their own. His success was not tempting them to do a bad thing, but rather tempting them to do a good thing without God. He got them thinking *lipnay Elohim* was just a temporary thing. They could just grow out of it and become like gods themselves. Theoretically, gods don't need *lipnay Elohim*, I guess. How easy was it for the Serpent? I think we often do a disservice by telling the story in a way that implies God had some other business elsewhere to attend to. No, Satan did his thing right in front of God's face. On that day, nothing was stopping Adam and Eve from looking up, *lipnay Elohim*. God was right there. All Eve or Adam had to do was look up into God's adoring eyes. When Eve did that 10,000 times out of 10,000 before, she would get this massive hit of acceptance dopamine. God always adored her. Always. God was so proud of her. All she had to do was ask God for wisdom.

But then? She didn't. If that's true, then her 'sin' was she didn't keep looking into the adoring eyes of God. Her sin was the inaugural "grabbing illusions of control," but definitely not the last. She shifted from *lipnay Elohim* to *lipnay fruit*, *lipnay Eve's feelings*, and *lipnay Satan*. It was a subtle but wildly significant shift. I do it all the time.

Kathryn Tanner suggests what led to this first sin was Adam and Eve taking the God-gifts for granted...

> "...and failed to realize how they could be lost through their own inattention to their cultivation, for example by failing to draw upon them, turning away from them, and therefore leading lives inappropriate to them...The result is a human life that has turned its back on the presence of God in its meaning for human life, a human life that has made God absent to itself, for all intents and purposes, through blindness to God's presence."[18]

She adds,

> "Because [we] are not God, [we] come to image God only by receiving what is not [our] own. In virtue of being received in something not itself divine, what [we] have from God does not exist in [us] in the way it does in God, in perfect or

divine fashion—fully, unchangeably, and without susceptibility of loss."[19]

Eve and Adam learned the hard way. What happened next? Way back in the 4th century, theologian Athanasius taught when Adam and Eve turned their backs on God's face and even began to do their own thing, the Spirit was taken away from them, and they were functionally disinherited, and orphaned. Yet, the God of grace stands ready to receive them again, give them the Spirit, and call them sons and daughters again.[20]

After the Fall

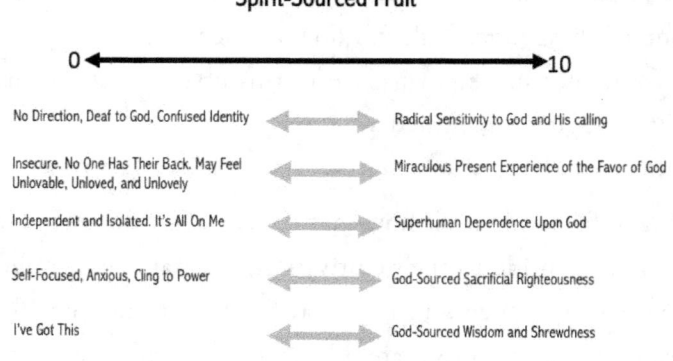

Spirit-Sourced Fruit

0 ← ———————————————————— → 10

No Direction, Deaf to God, Confused Identity	Radical Sensitivity to God and His calling
Insecure. No One Has Their Back. May Feel Unlovable, Unloved, and Unlovely	Miraculous Present Experience of the Favor of God
Independent and Isolated. It's All On Me	Superhuman Dependence Upon God
Self-Focused, Anxious, Cling to Power	God-Sourced Sacrificial Righteousness
I've Got This	God-Sourced Wisdom and Shrewdness

Here is the *Spirit-Sourced Fruit* chart again, remember? "0-10". "Ten" is what Eve and Adam experienced with God all the time until they didn't. When the Spirit was removed from them, their experience of their former empowering relationship with God likely dropped precipitously. I believe their experience shifted to the five descriptors to the left.

First, before the Big Mess, Eve, and Adam each understood who they were with God and each other and knew what they were to accomplish together. But then, after the Fall, "zero", they were confused, directionless, purposeless, and had fractured their life-giving relationship with God.

Before the Fall, Eve and Adam felt the favor of God all the time. When the Spirit was withdrawn from them, they felt unlovable, unloved, and unlovely. Fear, anxiety, and shame kicked in—all new to Eve and Adam. So much for the supposed "knowledge of good and evil." It was very dramatic and a lie. Nowhere do we read God's assessment of her changed. But you couldn't tell her that.

She reacted by desperately covering herself and hiding from God behind a tree (Gen 3:7-8)—really?

Before Satan's lies, Eve and Adam existed naturally dependent upon God. Adam and Eve fell from life-giving dependence upon God to an isolating, shame-riddled independence from God and each other.

Before the Fall, I strongly suspect Eve and Adam would have given their lives for each other. It was God's righteousness coursing through their veins. Afterward, each became concerned with his or her own well-being and security over the needs of the other, a little or a lot. Eve *"gave some [fruit] to her husband, who was with her, and he ate it" (3:6)*. The statement is stark and emotionless. Eve knowingly sentenced Adam to death. She would never have done that if God-sourced righteousness was sweeping through her veins.

Lastly, before the Fall, if something came up they were not familiar with in the process of BFMFRSing, Eve and Adam could simply, with no loss of face, look up into God's face and ask what they should do. Post-Fall? They are on their own. Time to take the so-called "Knowledge of Good and Evil" for a spin—not that it will do either of them any good at all.

Eve was, at one point in time, the ideal biblical woman. Nothing that happened can take that title away from her. She alone fully experienced self-identity and worth, feeling lovable, lovely, and loved more and longer than any other woman ever has. This is how I like to imagine her. Eve, filled with this fullness of God, was more "woman" than any other "woman" ever. She beautifully radiated her relationship with God. She would have been known for her amazing grace and sensitivity to God and Adam. Adam would have sought her out for her godly wisdom. She flowered with the confidence that God was so proud of her all the time. She didn't need to prove anything to God,

Adam, or herself. Righteous? Oh yes. If ever needed, she would have sacrificed her well-being for her husband.

...until everything changed.

How Can Daughters of the Most High, Post-Fall, Possibly Experience This Spirit-Sourced Fruit?

Now, fast forward many generations from the days of Eve and Adam to the period of the Israelites. None of these six amazing daughters of Eve in this book had the perspective of Eve Pre-Fall. None of them could imagine what it would have felt like to know beyond knowing what God feels toward them as they are. We will start our journey with two women from the chaotic and anti-*lipnay Elohim* period of the Judges. Each would have found themselves as women in a largely patriarchal world. You think you have seen troubles? When God finds them, none of these glorious women would have been expected to become or do much. But then, God...

How can these daughters of the Most High possibly pull this off when the most perfect woman didn't? Or maybe a better question? What can we learn from their struggles and successes today? Curious?

Engage Questions:

1. What have you learned that you didn't know before?

2. Was Eve the ideal woman? Thoughts?

3. As you look at the "Spirit-Sourced Fruit" chart, share your thoughts.

4. Think of Eve Pre-Fall. Describe what it would have been like to <u>not</u> have a critical inner voice.

---

1. Milne, Pamela, "Genesis from Eve's Point of View."

2. Asher-Perrin, "*Barbie*," para. 11.

3. But it turns out, Adam and Eve were well over their heads. Or were they? Looking back, from the beginning, now we can see that subduing and ruling was only to be achieved as they were more and more dependent upon God, God's wisdom, and strength. If Adam and Eve were acting as dynamic dependent willing arms and agents of God, the Vegas odds would have dramatically shifted. Satan would have gone from -500 hands-down favorite to +500 underdog.

4. Brendtro, "Vision of Urie Bronfenbrenner."

5. This irrational love is not a function of our success or record. We Jesus-followers understand that Jesus purchased this effectual assurance for us 2000 years ago. It is ours. But, after thirty plus years of ministry, I have observed that too many Christians, women, and men equally, struggle to experience this day to day. Many haven't felt it for a long time. The Spirit can make regular, shamed, doubt-riddled, failure-prone people like us grasp the limitless love of God for us as we are right now, not as we should be or could be. This is far better than anyone else has ever treated us. This is way beyond what we deserve. We can never get there through reason, apologetics, or even theology classes. We can't just 'choose' to feel it. Too good to believe? The Holy Spirit can change "If it is too good to believe, then it must not be true," to "It is too good to believe, but for some reason I actually believe and am beginning to experience it."

6. David Arredondo, "Attunement." "Infants do not have the capacity to self-regulate their internal emotional states. Instead, they rely on caregivers to constantly attune to the moment to moment shifts in their emotional states. When caregivers respond to infant's distress, they help to regulate their autonomic nervous system (ANS) by providing a feeling of safety, thereby slowing our heartbeat, curving the production of stress hormones, and bringing our physiology back to a state of calm."

7. Spooner, *Attachment-Focused Family Play Therapy*, 27. "Children raised in families with secure attachment patterns are often resilient and able to effectively navigate the ups and downs of healthy relationships and the world in general, largely because they can effectively regulate their emotions. Parents act as co-regulators for a child's emotions and help the child learn to internalize the ability to manage strong emotions." The quality of early parent/caregiver/child bonding, in particular through attunement, has been shown to influence the child's future self-concept, decision-making, emotion regulation, and behavior. Spooner writes that this is "a kinesthetic and emotional sensing of others knowing their rhythm, affect and experience by metaphorically being in their skin, and going beyond empathy to create a two-person experience of unbroken connectedness by providing a reciprocal affect and/or resonating response...Scientists will tell you that this is not just a game or a good thing. Infant attunement causes an explosion of powerful neural activity within the brain of the infant that connects them emotionally and psychically with their caregiver. If infants do not experience such regular attuning with their primary caregiver, "then their perceptions of themselves as lovable and acceptable will be impaired. They will develop negative beliefs of themselves that will negatively influence their ability to establish and maintain healthy relationships."(Spooner, *Attachment*, 30)

8. Biblically, the phrase *lipnay Elohim* has a very broad meaning. If you have an urgent request of God, you can "seek the face" of God (2 Sam 21:1). When Samuel's Hannah was deeply distressed, she turned to God. In 1 Sam 1:12, we are told that she earnestly prayed *lipnay Yahweh*. The image is that spiritually she got right up into his Holy face, eye-to-eye, face-to-face, and soul-to-soul. In her distress, she experienced a powerful emotional in-syncness with God. No doubt you have experienced such a connection with God once or twice. There is great power and healing there. Did someone do something bad to you? You go to the temple *lipnay Elohim* expecting that God will judge your case. You go face-to-face, in the Hebrew, "*paneh* to *paneh*" with the Judge (Dt 19:17, 25:9). Official oaths and business deals are also done up in the face of God (Gen 27:7). Corporate celebrations of thanksgiving are done in God's face (Dt 12:7, 18). Are you ashamed? Burdened by guilt. You go *lipnay Elohim* with your confession and your guilt offerings (Hos 5:15, Ex 18:12). I get it. You hurt someone badly, a text won't do. You need to see their eyes and they see yours. Are you feeling isolated, alone, and vulnerable? You can find connection and peace in the face of God (Ps 42:2). Soul-to-soul. It is true with God and us. Do you need capacity to push back against Satan, to BFMFRS, or fight that nasty critical inner voice? You need to "seek God's face *all the time*." (Ps 105:4).

9. In Tanner, *Christ the Key*, 28.

10. Siegel, "Attunement."

11. Marks-Tarlow, "Interpersonal Neurobiology," 219-236.

12. Centers for Disease Control, "Adolescents."

13. I speak to churches often and I am so tired of hearing that discipleship is "becoming more like Jesus," or "doing what Jesus would do." Can't we hear the shadowy backdrop of residual independence in those way too popular statements? Isn't it better to see discipleship as "becoming more and more *dependent* upon Jesus and his Spirit?" But there's that nasty four-letter word again, "dependent."

14. Let me unpack this a bit. What was one of the main things that drove Jesus to take on flesh? The most obvious answer is that he loved others, "Be like-minded, having the same love." That love for others didn't have even the slightest smell of selfish ambition, no ulterior motive, "Do nothing out of selfish ambition or vain conceit, but in humility consider others better than yourselves. Each of you should look not only to your own interests, but also to the interests of others." Think about this for a moment. Paul says that Jesus did it because he "considered others better than himself." To be clear, we are not in any way better than Him. That is just a way to describe his drive to *taipenoo* himself. *Taipenoo* refers to Jesus humbling, humiliating, and abasing himself (2:3, 8). Why? He does it for needy others, like me, like you. He loves us that much. As you can see, the righteousness of Jesus has a sacrificial "other" focus to it. It can be very costly, as it was in Jesus' case. This is what God-sourced righteousness looks like.

15. Olley, "Righteousness," 307-315.

16. Biblical righteous actions are geared to bringing about "prosperity, benefit, equal rights for all subjects, including freedom from external oppression and deliverance from enemies...[It reflects] a concern for the well-being of one's fellows." Olley, "Righteousness," 309-312. This is not just a New Testament thing. In the Psalms, we see this inherent righteousness of God.

17. Waltke, *Proverbs*, 85.

18. "Humans have the image of God only by clinging to what they are not – that divine image itself – becoming attached to it not merely physically but in every way possible for them – ideally with purity of attention, full commitment, and intense love." A person "images God only by participating in God, that is, by continuing to receive what it has from God. To be a creature just means to lead an insufficient life of oneself, to lead a continually borrowed life." Augustine wrote about our post-fall need for dependence, "Man is not so constituted that he would be able, when once created, to perform any good deed by his own powers . . . All his good action consists in his being turned to him by whom he has been made, and in his becoming, by his creator's power, just, faithful, wise, and blessed always." In Tanner, *Christ the Key* , 28.

19. Tanner, *Christ the Key* , 7.

20. In Tanner, *Christ the Key* , 27.

Chapter Three

The Woman In the Shadows

Let us explore the stories of two amazing women, relative contemporaries, only forty years apart.[1]

The biblical term for their unfortunate situation is harsh and cold. They were barren. That carried with it huge social and personal stigmas.

Most likely, at one point, both were happy young brides looking forward to the next step of motherhood: raising a large Israelite family, becoming matriarchs of their tribe, and entering the circle of other like-minded women who had full tents. But then they realized they could not get pregnant.

This places Hannah and the unnamed mother of Samson alongside Sarah, Rebekah, Rachel, and Leah, six renowned women of Israel who were barren when God entered their stories. God does not leave them there.

It's a big deal. Science has found even today, young infertile women tend to experience anxiety, panic, anger, sadness, emotional numbness, or even hopelessness.[2]

Today, there are technologies that can help. But those too are a risk. What if they fail after so much money is spent? There is adoption or foster care, both very good things, but it was not the dream.

When God encounters these two biblical women, their societal shame will be palpable. There would be conscious or subconscious pressure from their husbands and families, an overwhelming sense of worthlessness and anxiety that they were being cursed by God for some unknown indiscretion, and that unfulfilled yearning for a child of their own.

I imagine women like them rightly complaining to God. "If you are up there and really care about your daughters, wouldn't you show us mercy and *open our wombs*?" It is an ancient phrase, but we get it. The cry would not be too dissimilar from "My God, my God, why have you forsaken me?"

Why do we begin our journey with these two unfortunate ladies? I can't think of a better pair to put the compassionate heart of God on full display. Hannah and the unnamed mother of Samson represent those whom God innately pursues: the most vulnerable, the disadvantaged, the helpless, and the barren. God loves those who feel unlovable, unloved, and unlovely, then, and today. God showers honor upon the dishonored and glory upon the shamed. And then, when they look up and surprisingly find themselves in the loving arms of God, *lipnay Elohim*[3], it is there that a redeemed "Eve-ness" emerges that takes their breath away.

These are the stories of two truly amazing daughters of the Most High. This chapter is about the unnamed wife of Manoah. But I will begin with an important teaser about Hannah, the topic of the next chapter.

Context: The Two Husbands

The Bible begins, rightly or wrongly, with the two women's husbands.
"There was a certain man...Elkanah" (1 Sam 1:1).

Elkanah (1 Sam 1) was Hannah's husband. The author makes the point that Elkanah loved Hannah (1:6), whose name means "Grace", even though she was infertile. Elkanah, Hannah, oh, and his second wife, "Beautiful Flowing Hair"—the plot thickens—lived in the hill country north of present-day Jerusalem.

The Bible notes they are devout Israelites of the tribe of Ephraim. It seems they regularly travel to worship God at the Tabernacle in Shiloh. Their actions contrast with the abysmal lack of corporate devotion to God in the land of Israel during the time of the Judges. Hold that thought. As we will see in the next chapter, Hannah has learned to depend on the intimate *lipnay Elohim*. This tells us so much about her. God has a high purpose for her. She will become the mother of the king-maker Samuel.

But, before we dig into Hannah's amazing story, we will go back a few chapters in Judges, a long day's journey, and maybe forty years earlier to meet another very special lady.

In Judges 13, we are introduced to Manoah, of the tribe of Dan, who lived in the hill country at the eastern edge of the Soreq Valley, southwest of modern Jerusalem. The Philistines owned and ran the luscious and fertile Soreq Valley, bullying Israel to hide up in the hills. Someone described Israel as frightened mice hiding from the dangerous cats that roamed the valleys.

Manoah's wife was also barren. Note the author uses the very same introductory phrase for her husband.

"There was a certain man...Manoah" (Judges 13:2).

Manoah and his wife were eventually the parents of the hairy Judge Samson. Manoah likely means "resting one." I imagine as an infant, Manoah didn't cry much and, fortunately for his mother, slept well. Maybe today we would call him "Chill."

The Period of the Judges

For context, I should say a little more about the period of the judges. Joshua and First Samuel create the bookends for the period. Judges covers the chaotic time between the death of Joshua and the establishment of the Tent of Meeting at Shiloh and the beginning of the Israeli monarchy, well over 400 years.[4]

The often-overlooked key to the book of Judges is what happens in Shiloh, a city near the modern West Bank city of Khirbet Seilun, in the hill country twenty miles north of modern Jerusalem. At the end of Joshua, the Tent of Meeting was set up in Shiloh (Josh 18-19). This was long before the temple was established in Jerusalem. All the disparate tribes of Israel were commanded to go there to worship God three times a year.

There they were to be remembered by the Lord, recapture their stories, and be God's people again. In our terminology, there they were to look up, *lipnay Elohim,*[5] and be reconnected to God's Spirit. There, the priest would tell them about Yahweh, about God's compassion, mercy, justice, and faithfulness. There they were to access the power of God needed for men and women to be righteous, spiritually aware, and dependent. There they would become one people again—many tribes, but a single loaf. Three times a year, they were to corporately gather and answer God's original Edenic question, "Where are you?" (Gen 3:9).

So, what happened at Shiloh during the 400 years of the Judges?
Nothing.

Unfortunately, there is no record of Israel gathering in Shiloh to worship
God even once. There is a single reference to an annual festival there, but it
sounds more pagan than Torahic. We won't see an *active* Tent of Meeting
until the next book, Samuel—until Elkanah and Hannah.

It is no surprise then that "everyone was doing what was right in their
own eyes" (Judges 17:6 and 21:25). As I said in the last chapter, being in
the presence of God is critical for post-Eden humanity, who is grasping at
illusions of control and disconnected from *lipnay Elohim*.

It sounds so modern, doesn't it? By Chill's (i.e., Manoah's) time, Israel
saw little reason to go to Shiloh to worship God. More likely, they just
don't think about God or Shiloh much anymore. The consequence is they
are beginning to look like all the other tribes in the land. I wonder if this
is the epitaph of the modern Western church as well.

How deeply entrenched was this spiritual barrenness?

> "Then the LORD raised up judges, who saved them out of the
> hand of those who plundered them. Yet they did not listen to
> their judges, for they whored after other gods and bowed down
> to them. They soon turned aside from the way in which their
> fathers had walked, who had obeyed the commandments of the
> LORD, and they did not do so. Whenever the LORD raised up
> judges for them, the LORD was with the judge, and he saved
> them from the hand of their enemies all the days of the judge.
> For the LORD was moved to pity by their groaning because
> of those who afflicted and oppressed them. But whenever the
> judge died, they turned back and were more corrupt than their
> fathers, going after other gods, serving them, and bowing down
> to them. They did not drop any of their practices or their
> stubborn ways" (Judges 2:16-19 ESV).

Check out a panoply of self-oriented verbs independent of God. They did not listen, they whored after, they bowed down, they turned aside. You see the problem.

How bad had it devolved? In five of the earlier "judge-cycles"[6] we read that Israel would at last come to a point when they realized "doing what was right in their own eyes" was only making matters worse (c.f., Judges 3:9, 15, 4:3, 6:6, 10:10). They would swallow their pride and cry out to God in need, and I would add, in shame.

This side of Eden is where God finds each of us. The Israelites were largely deaf to God, not sure where they stood with others, leaning toward being independent persons, arguably more concerned with their own well-being than others, and lacking the God-sourced wisdom that could bring shalom (i.e., peace) to the people.

Things had deteriorated so much in this "judge cycle," that no one was even crying out to God. Maybe they could all be categorized as "Manoah"—i.e., chill, unaware of the danger, of the breach with their Creator, of what they were missing. Maybe they just didn't remember God and the previous rescues? Maybe the God of Abraham and Moses had been relegated to just bedtime tales for children. I wonder what Eve and Adam would say to them if they could.

Like Adam and Eve immediately after the fall, they will not look up, *lipnay Elohim*. They do not access the Heaven-born spiritual awareness and sensitivity, God-sourced wisdom, or biblical righteousness, where people are more concerned about the well-being of others, particularly the most vulnerable among them. Tragic.

In a word, perhaps much like these two women, they too were barren.

How could we categorize Israel's relationship with God during that time? I imagine they would see God like the sign on many buses, "In case of emergency, break glass!" Let me put it this way, it would seem a spiritual *rigor mortis* had set in.

I am not judging. I can relate to "doing what is right in my own eyes." We all do it. It seems hard for us humans to expect God to care enough to intervene on a regular basis. Tragically, this is what defined Chill's Israel.

Paul got it right a thousand years later, "All creation groans." Apart from God's empowerment, society devolved into a battlefield where only the strongest might survive and the vulnerable became even more vulnerable.

Speaking of the vulnerable, I want to say a word about how women fared in the four hundred years of Judges. Generally, very poorly. There are a few women who stand out. In Judges 1:12-15, we read of Achsah, the daughter of the great General Caleb. Wreaking with *chutzpah*, she "urges" (Heb: *'sut'*- incited) her father for a sizable marriage dowry, a field. Then she returns to the table and requests more. In response to her shocking second request, he gives her the valuable upper and lower springs in the Negev (Judges 1:9-15). This was a risky female initiative. She pulls it off.

There is also the outstanding Judge Deborah and the little-known Ya'el. I will say more about them later.

But for the most part, as we would expect, the women of patriarchal Israel, particularly during this ungodly era, are treated very poorly: overlooked, underappreciated, sometimes brutalized, and, with very few exceptions, dismissed.

I am not sure how this hits you. Research has shown even today, in the most liberal and progressive nations, women's self-esteem significantly lags behind men's. There is no modern nation where that is not the case. You may or may not be aware of sexism and the effect it has on your gender, but it is all around you.[7]

In Israel, during the time of the Judges, it was likely even worse. Consider a trauma/self-esteem scale from '0-10', with '10' being severe trauma and very low self-esteem and '0' being high esteem and no trauma at all. On the '10' side of the scale would be the terrible violence and horrific absurdity of the human sacrifice of Jephthah's daughter (Judges 11:29–40), the gang rape of the Levite's voiceless, nameless concubine (Judges 19:25–29), and the kidnapping and forced marriage of the daughters of Shiloh (Judges 21:20–23).

On the opposite side of the scale might be the respect and reverence afforded to Deborah. The rest of the stories we will look at are about women who are on the debilitating side of the trauma/self-esteem scale somewhere. You may feel more comfortable placing them at a '3' or a '5', but to one degree or another, these women, daughters of Eve, feel somewhat silenced and oppressed relative to their male counterparts. It is just the way things were.

But all of this is how they were before God intervened.

The Mother of Samson

Meet Chill's wife and the mother of the great judge, Samson. It may surprise you, as you read her story, that she is included in one ancient rabbi's list of twenty-three truly upright and righteous women who came forth from Israel.[8]

To be sure, that is not where God finds her. She appears to be the most silenced of all the women we will consider. Yet God knows exactly what she is capable of and the honor she will receive.

Often, in the Bible, it's the gaps that are the most interesting. "Gaps" are those things you would expect to happen or to be said in the text but are not.

In this case, we are not even given her name, only her husband's, Chill (Manoah). Often, that reflects the character wasn't so memorable. At this point, she was the societally disappointing barren wife of an unlikable man, Chill. The later Babylonian rabbis came to her rescue, however, and ordained her Zlelponi.[9] We will use this name for her as well.

Some suggest her name comes from the Hebrew '*zll*' meaning "shadows." I think that says a lot.

"There was a certain man of Zorah, of the tribe of the Danites, whose name was Manoah. And his wife was barren and had no children. And the angel of the LORD appeared to the woman and said to her, "Behold, you are barren and have not borne children, but you shall conceive and bear a son. Therefore, be careful and drink no wine or strong drink, and eat nothing unclean, for behold, you shall conceive and bear a son. No razor shall come upon his head, for the child shall be a Nazirite to God from the womb, and he shall begin to save Israel from the hand of the Philistines." Then the woman came and told her husband, "A man of God came to me, and his appearance was like the appearance of the angel of God, very awesome. I did not ask him where he was from, and

he did not tell me his name, but he said to me, 'Behold, you shall conceive and bear a son. So then drink no wine or strong drink, and eat nothing unclean, for the child shall be a Nazirite to God from the womb to the day of his death.'" (Jud 13:2-7)

This is probably a little unfair but allow me some leeway. When the angel meets "Shadows," she seems awkwardly silent. She asks no questions. She shows no emotion or reaction.

Perhaps this is another intentional gap, but I wonder why the author chose not to develop her humanity more. Even before that, I find it curious she is never shown praying to God to "open her womb"—like Hannah (who we will see shortly). She is missing normal human reactions to distressful situations. Her character comes across to me as a bit two-dimensional.

Maybe the likely male editor doesn't feel it is worthy of being included in the record. Perhaps, and more likely, Zlelponi has learned in patriarchal Israel it is better to be quiet.

The later Greek philosopher Pericles (495-429 BCE) unfortunately wrote, "The highest glory for a woman is to be spoken of in neither praise nor blame." Maybe for Shadows, it wasn't about glory; rather, it was the safest path as well.

I suspect also there is a parallel being presented between Shadows and Israel. Neither seem to expect God to have much to do with them anymore. In such a context, accepting the status quo and living silently under oppression may be seen as better than speaking up and drawing unwanted attention to yourself. Perhaps Shadows had decided, like many other women of her day, to remain in the shadows.

If I were to stage this scene, Shadows would be cast as an immature, vulnerable, and insecure teenage girl, at most 16 years old. In ancient Israel, girls were usually betrothed immediately after their first period (12-13 years of age) and married a year or so later. The betrothal would have been arranged by her father with no legal consent needed from the bride. In our Western minds, this practice seems so troubling. The bride's dowry, which reflected her cultural worth, was negotiated by the men (fathers, brothers, and male guardians) largely based on the girl's virginity and her expected productivity of children for her new husband. That was her main role in Israelite society.

Her husband, Chill, would most likely be quite a bit older, perhaps in his late 20s or even early 30s. The actual marriage would not take place until the groom could prove to his father that he could support a wife. So Chill was likely older and more confident than his child bride.

By the time of the angelic visitation in Judges 13, Shadows *should* have been a mother. That was the expectation for women in Israel, to bear their husband's many children, hopefully boys. Her inability to have children would be noticed quickly by the entire village and would become a shameful stigma for her to bear. It would have been quite hard for an adolescent. From what we are learning about Chill, he wasn't one to be encouraging.

Perhaps long before the angelic visitation, this young teenager, due to no fault of her own, had already become a silenced shadow, no longer a valued partner, just a burden, another mouth to feed. Wouldn't that explain another "gap"—her apparent lack of prayer to God for a child?

So now, let the fun begin. God has not forgotten Shadows. In fact, I believe God is much more interested in her story than Chill's. Our first clue? The angel appears, not to Chill but to Shadows.

"The angel of the LORD appeared to her and said, 'You are sterile and childless, but you are going to conceive and have a son.'" (Judges 13:3)

This would have been seen as a blatant cultural offense to Chill. We have a modern phrase about "poking the bear." According to an urban dictionary, it is to act in such a way that has a good, but not definite, chance of causing trouble. You can poke a bear once and maybe get away with it, but if you keep poking him, he's going to get angry.

I counted four times—maybe more—that God poked the bear. God had this guy's number. Getting Chill rattled is what we used to call in Louisiana "lagniappe." Lagniappe is the word for a bonus gift given to a customer—something over the top, unexpected, or gratuitous that makes him or her smile. Restoring Zlelponi to her lost honor in Israel was the goal. Poking the bear is just God's lagniappe.

Back to the story. The angel tells silent Zlelponi that she is not a disappointment—not to God anyway. She will conceive and give birth to a very special son. The angel of God gives her a series of somewhat technical instructions. He must be raised as a Nazarite, meaning he was to never have any intoxicating drink, never cut his hair, and remain undefiled by not touching a dead thing.

The angel surprisingly adds he should not eat any unclean food. Why did that even need to be mentioned? That was the law for all Israelite men and women already. Likely, it had to be said because it wasn't the practice of the Israelites during the period of the Judges. Remember? Everyone was doing what was right in their own eyes. Including Chill and Zlelponi, presumably.

Once again, there is a noticeable absence of the expression of normal human emotions in Zlelponi. While she will describe the angel to her husband as "frightening" (13:6—a better translation than "awesome"), her actions seem to be out of sync with what one would expect.

Others who were in the presence of an angel exhibit normal human fear (Zechariah, Lk 1:12; Mary, Lk 1:29; Isaiah, Isa 6:1-4; Balaam, Num 22:31-32; King Belshazzar, Dan 5:6). Zlelponi just says nothing. She asks nothing. She doesn't even need his name. She seems to casually receive the message and then goes to tell Chill. I think this poor, stigmatized woman was more terrorized by Chill than afraid of the angel.

How did Chill deal with the cultural 'poke the bear' from this? What appeared to be a disrespectful stranger?

> *"Then Manoah prayed to the LORD and said, 'My Lord, please let the man of God whom you sent come again to us and teach us what we are to do with the child who will be born.'"* (Judges 13:8)

Don't just accept Chill's entreaty as true devotional prayer. There is good prayer and not-so-good prayer. Remember when I spoke about gaps? What is missing from this picture? Chill has just heard God is opening his wife's womb. A miracle in a land of very sparse miracles.

C'mon man. Even a slightly more spiritually sensitive guy would have offered God a prayer of thanks. A better husband would have expressed some joy on behalf of his wife's good news. Right? It's just not there. This prayer is void of thanks or respect. I now wonder if the name "Manoah" has another connotation other than "chill." What's Hebrew for passive-aggressive, sexist, or just flat "out of sync" with God?

Jewish Midrash piles on, creatively reporting how Chill tosses his wife under the proverbial bus.[10]

"Until now, I heard from my wife, but women are not qualified to teach, and I do not rely on what they say. Let your words come. I want to hear from your mouth, for I do not believe what she says; perhaps she may have changed something while speaking, omitted something, or added something."

They go on to describe Chill as an 'ignoramus' who had not even learned Scripture, while his spouse was one of the twenty-three truly upright and righteous women who came forth from Israel. Today, we might say he was a Neanderthal. Chill wants a man-to-man—or a Divine-to-man chat. God wants Zlelponi to be honored more than she has ever experienced in her life.

I love it.

Bear poke #2. This is one of those glorious moments in the Bible when we get to really see God's celestial sense of humor. On the surface, God honors passive-aggressive Chill's request for a testosterone parlay—sort of.

There is another visit, but the angel is once again sent back to Chill's wife. As I said, it seems God is far more interested in Zlelponi than Chill. That will leave a mark.

Here is my expanded interpretive translation of verses 9-10. "God read between the lines of Chill's sexist concerns and begged to disagree. In her honor, the angel was publicly dispatched to Zlelponi again. She was not used to receiving such an honor. Being fearful of what Chill might do, she anxiously ran to find him to let him know the man was back."

The editor displays Zlelponi's concern. After the first angelic appearance, Zlelponi casually went to Chill and told Chill about him. Very calm, generic

Hebrew verbs. After the second appearance, the woman is reported as urgently scurrying (Hebrew: *rutz mahar*) to Chill, making sure he heard the angel was back.

I assume Zlelponi is naturally afraid of Chill's possible reaction. I get the sense Chill is not used to being treated this way. But neither is the angel of the Lord.

I am a modern man with modern sensibilities, to be sure, so the lens I am bringing to this text may be culturally skewed. However, Chill is not coming across as a very likable character—at all. Why do I say that? Let's start off with what reaction we might expect when one sees an angel of God. Abraham ran from his tent door and bowed himself to the earth before angel visitors (Gen 18:2-15). The verb to bow down (Hebrew-*chawah*) is a very strong word reflecting deep submission to one in authority. Lot rose to meet the angels and bowed down (Gen 19:1-22) with his face on the ground (Hebrew: *chawah*). Even Balaam 'bowed low and fell facedown' (Num 22:31-35). Joshua (Josh 5:13-15) fell facedown to the ground in reverence (Hebrew-*chawah*). In Judges 2, the people heard the message of the angel and wept in repentance (Judges 2:1-4).

But not Chill, not nose-bent-out-of-joint, passive-aggressive, and sexist Chill.

When Chill came to the angel he said, "Are you the one who spoke to the woman?" There is a noticeable void of spiritual awareness in Chill. He has very little righteousness toward his wife or strangers. Zero fear of the Lord.

The angel curtly responds, "I am." Again, no bowing, no deference. Chill begins by asking the angel how they are to raise the boy. Honestly, I can think of a hundred other things I would have asked. This question had already been answered by the angel when he spoke to Zlelponi. I understand the angel's almost sarcastic response as, "I already spoke to your wife about all of that. Just ask her. Is there a problem?" Chill is indeed Samson's father. I heard a great quote. "The tree doesn't grow far from the apple."

Bear poke #3? Chill has another control gambit to play.

Manoah said to the angel of the LORD, "Please let us detain
you and prepare a young goat for you."

In that paganized Israelite culture, it was understood you gain some power over spiritual entities by 1) eating with them and 2) finding out their name. If they consent to dine with you, you are now, to some degree, allied with them. They have accepted your hospitality, and you are officially at peace. If they give you their name, you have the leverage of control over them. Knowing a name gives you power, they thought.

Well, the angel flatly turns Chill's offer of a meal down, a very public and offensive move in such a high-hospitality culture. This would have felt to Chill like a spit in his face.

"And the angel of the LORD said to Manoah, 'If you detain
me, I will not eat of your food. But if you prepare a burnt
offering, then offer it to the LORD.' (For Manoah did not
know that he was the angel of the LORD.)" (Judges 13:15-16)

Bear poke #4? Then the angel refuses to give Chill his name.

"Then Manoah inquired of the angel of the LORD, 'What is
your name, so that we may honor you when your word comes
true?' [The angel] replied, 'Why do you ask my name? It is
beyond understanding.'" (Judges 13:17-18)

This was not just some casual chit-chat. In Chill's mind, he was vying for some control, some advantage. It was not to be.

The angel had come to honor Zlelponi, not to put up with Chill's arrogance.

Chill does make an offering to the Lord, but he does not expect what happens. He had severely misread the room.

"Then Manoah took a young goat, together with the grain offering, and sacrificed it on a rock to the LORD. And the LORD did an amazing thing while Manoah and his wife watched: As the flame blazed up from the altar toward heaven, the angel of the LORD ascended in the flame. Seeing this, Manoah and his wife fell with their faces to the ground. When the angel of the LORD did not show himself again to Manoah and his wife, Manoah realized that it was the angel of the LORD. 'We are doomed to die!' he said to his wife. 'We have seen God!'" (Judges 13:19-22)

Now it is time for Chill to feel what being vulnerable is all about. His heart is struck down with fear. Maybe he is beginning to realize his vulnerable wife has a righteous protector who has her back and who has come to bring her glory and a new name.

Ok, drum roll. So far, we have seen and heard very little from Zlelponi. Until now, she has survived in Chill's harsh shadow. But it is time for her to move out of the shadows and into Hebrew lore. She, not Chill, knows what she is to do. Old Testament scholar J. Cheryl Exum rightly observes that Zlelponi does finally sense something "otherworldly."[11]

Spirit-Sourced Fruit

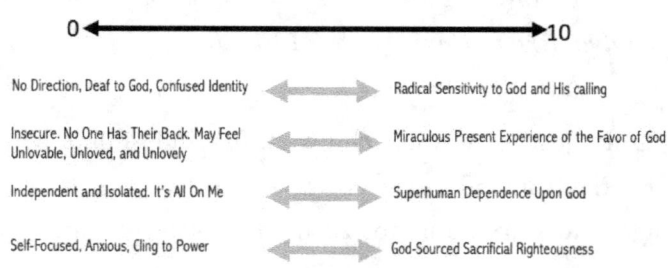

On our *Spirit-Sourced Fruit* Spectrum, the first trait, or better, the first empowerment of God's Spirit, was a radical sensitivity to God and His calling. This is that inner, God-sourced capacity to recognize it is indeed God who is speaking, and the Lord of the Heavens actually has

your back. God specifically wants her to do something special. It is a beautiful thing to see. Often, these individuals can miraculously hear God when no one else does.

I think of Mary, the mother of Jesus. Mary was famously God-aware and willing. An emissary of God told her out of the blue,

> *"The Holy Spirit will come upon you, and the power of the Most High will overshadow you; therefore, the child to be born will be called holy—the Son of God."*

Filled with this God-sourced radical awareness, Mary responds,

> *"Behold, I am the servant of the Lord; let it be to me according to your word." And the angel departed from her. (Luke 1:26-38)*

In a similar emotional space, Zlelponi also plunges in. Even though she is somehow aware it is God's voice speaking to her through the angel, she is not afraid. She feels, dare I say, more honored than perhaps she has ever felt in her short life. She leaves the episode fully aware of what God would have her do. Shadows, the barren one, the shamed one, is now the beloved of God and is filled with new life.

Listen to the unsilenced Zlelponi *lipnay Elohim.*

> *"But his wife answered, 'If the LORD had meant to kill us, he would not have accepted a burnt offering and grain offering from our hands, nor shown us all these things or now told us this.' The woman gave birth to a boy and named him Samson. He grew and the LORD blessed him." (Judges 13:23-24)*

From that point on in Judges, whenever we see Chill, we almost always see Zlelponi as an equal partner (Judges 14:2, 3, 4, 5, 6, 9, 16:31). God did more than just open Zlelponi's womb once. We are told in 16:31 that Samson had brothers. Way to go, Shadows.

It is a noticeable transformation. When God found her, I believe she was traumatized a little or a lot. She had been silenced and learned to bury her emotions. She, like so many other women, had learned to swallow her shame.

The Joy Luck Club by Amy Tan is a book about four Chinese American matriarchs' struggle for 'worth'. Each lived in the misogynistic society of mid-20th-century China. Each woman had suffered abuses, disappointments, betrayals, and humiliations at the hands of others (men and women) that they had no social power to fight against. In their context, they looked to secular Buddhism for answers—for some hope. But Buddhism tragically offers little to vulnerable women.

An-Mei had accepted her lot but came to realize that was part of her problem. I wonder if this reflects Zlelponi before God entered her picture. An-Mei's mother had this advice.

> "An-Mei, have you seen the turtle that lives in the pond?...This turtle feeds on our thoughts," said my mother. "I learned this one day, when I was your age, and [my mother] said I could no longer be a child. She said I could not shout, or run, or sit on the ground to catch crickets. I could not cry if I was disappointed. I had to be silent and listen to my elders...That night...I sat by the pond, looking into the water. And because I was weak, I began to cry. Then I saw this turtle swimming to the top and his beak was eating my tears as soon as they touched the water. The turtle said, 'I have eaten your tears, and this is why I know your misery. But I must warn you. If you cry, your life will always be sad...It is useless to cry. Your tears do not wash away your sorrows. They feed someone else's joy. And that is why you must learn to swallow your tears.'"[11]

This is *not* what Zlelponi did. The moral of her tale is *not* to swallow or even stop swallowing your tears. It is *not* to put on your big girl panties and stop putting up with society's rubbish that is preventing women from being in the dance.

Here is what I learned from Zlelponi. Child of the Most High, no matter what has been done to you, what you have done, or what you can't do, whether it is your fault or not, none of that affects how your heavenly Father feels toward you right now. You may have come to believe you are a disappointment, that God can't or won't use you, or that He does not have your back. Nothing could be further from the truth.

If you are a Christian and are reading this right now, that tells me God is certainly not through with you. If God were, it would be a disgraceful, unloving act to keep you here on earth and prevent you from experiencing the fullness of the Lord God that Jesus purchased for you 2000 years ago. Are you following me? Why would God keep you here unless there was something terribly important—something that required your unique gifts, personality, and history to accomplish—some heroic narrative in which you are called to do your part in redeeming the Eve narrative, a little or a lot?

God is willing to go into the darkest shadows to raise up the Beloved. Zlelponi was so beaten up she couldn't or wouldn't run to God. So, God came down to her, sought her out, and spoke life into her womb. God still does this today.

Summary

In the end, Chill and Zlelponi reflect the warp and woof of Israel of the day. They were the people of God. It said so on their business cards, but what did it really mean? Particularly to the most vulnerable? The worship of God had become watered down by paganism and superstition. Very few, including Zlelponi, it would seem, even went to Shiloh to worship God. The memory of God and God's promises to His people had long been suppressed, forgotten, or just ignored. Maybe they were mythical bedtime stories—the entertaining antics of Moses, Joshua, and Caleb—just Disney movies for entertainment—super action figures under the tree.

Zlelponi is not immune to the influence of her culture. Even after her legit God encounter, Zlelponi will still name her boy after the sun god of the local temple at Beth Shemesh. Habits are habits.

Tragically, Samson (i.e., Sunny Boy) will not fully rally Israel. He never leads Israel to battle, like the other judges. Israel is never inspired to follow. Unlike Deborah, Samson shows virtually zero God-sourced wisdom. He will never experience a military victory—like Gideon, Jephthah, Deborah, and Caleb. All his actions are personal, with arguably the possible exception of his last tragic act. Samson will sing songs of glory, but not to God, to his own antics alone.

Good news. A little over a millennium later, and 40 miles south, God will come to another childless woman, and she will give birth to the one—Jesus—the final '*Sonny* Boy' who will set His people free. He will be the anti-Samson. He is immersed in the Godhead perfectly. He is immersed in the grander story, the narrative of God's promises to Adam and Eve. He is not subject to His feelings and desires but subjugates them to the will of His God. "Not my will, but Your will be done!" He lives and dies for the sake of God's people. His death is on behalf of the people of God of all time. Through this second Samson, God will finally shape a single people out of the disparate tribes, a single worshipping loaf. This final Judge-Redeemer will set His people free from the present evil age (Gal 1:4). Through Him, we can see as He sees and truly feel compassion and love for 'others'.

Next Steps for all Zlelponi's

What can we all learn from Zlelponi's struggles and successes? Here's the thing I immediately consider, I am reminded that the critical, *shadowy* voice in my brain is not as powerful as I might have thought. Like Zlelponi, my "shadows" can also begin to be rewired by the power that exclusively comes from God. Before God found me, that destructive voice had me believe I was barren and unfixable in some way, unlovable, unlovely, and unloved. God's Spirit made me see and experience the shocking honor of a special relationship with God and gave me hope of becoming a source of life for others.

Allow me to speak to those remnant shadows in all our brains.

"Shadows, can't you see now that God loves you as you are, even when you are feeling unlovable, unloved, and unlovely? God's love is not affected by how others measure you or your value. It is not affected by how you see yourself. Mirrors often lie. This is who God is. As in creation, God's Spirit still hovers over the barrenness and chaos (Gen 1:2), speaking life into the shadows with unexpected fullness. Look up, *lipnay Elohim,* and be drenched in His pleasure in you again and again."

I want to encourage you to keep saying the *Simple Uncluttered Gospel*[12] twice a day for 45 days. I need to say it every day. Repetition is critical. It is a gospel presentation for that unreached mission field, your critical inner voice. Paul says the gospel is the power to believe. Believe what? Well, among many things, it is the power to believe that God truly loves you, even though you may currently feel unlovable, unloved, and unlovely. This world beats identity and worth out of us. We can quickly become "shadows."

We will look at Hannah next. She was like Zlelponi in some ways and very different in others. Hannah's story will sound so modern, so three-dimensional. Enjoy.

Engage Questions:

1. What did you learn that you did not know before? What difference does it make to you in your world today?

2. Where do you resonate with Zlelponi, "Shadows"?

3. If Jesus appeared to her, what might He say to her? What might He do?

---

1. Hannah was of the tribe of Ephraim and lived in the hill country north of present-day Jerusalem. Zlelponi was likely of the tribe of Dan and lived in the Sorek Valley southwest of present Jerusalem.

2. Sharma and Shrivastava. "Infertility."

3. The syntagm *Lipnay Elohim* is usually translated "In the presence of God." In our context, it refers to those moments when, by faith, you are gazing up into God's eyes and seeing just how much God adores you, is proud of you, is so excited that you are looking up, you feel so special—just like an infant gazing up at the eyes of his or her adoring mother. We discussed it more in the last chapter.

4. Jewish Rabbis believed that Samuel wrote all three books. Later scholarship speculates that this so-called "Deuteronomistic History" was compiled by a later editor(s) during the Babylonian exile. Either way, we would expect all three books to present a unified view of Israel's history and of course the important answer to the moral question, "Why did the exile need to happen?"

5. Look directly, by faith, into the face of God.

6. God's sending of judges to Israel seemed to follow a fourfold cycle: 1) the Israelites do what is evil in the sight of the Lord, 2) God allows the nation to be conquered and oppressed by a neighboring nation, 3) the people cry out to God, and 4) God sends a judge to deliver the Israelites. The cycle then repeats after the judge dies.

7. A recent massive 2015 study of 48 nations that reflects a broad cross section of cultural differences in socioeconomic, sociodemographic, gender-equality, and cultural value indicators, concluded that a woman's self-esteem "an individual's subjective evaluation of his or her worth as a person" was universally lower than a man's. In fact, there is no country where that is not the case. Bleidorn, et al. "Age and Gender," 396-410.

8. Kadari, "Wife of Manoach."

9. Kadari, "Wife of Manoach."

10. Kadari, "Wife of Manoach."

11. Tan, *Joy Luck Club*, 243-4.

12. Simple   Uncluttered   Gospel   bookmarks   are   available   at https://gospel-app.com/product/women-simple-uncluttered-gospel-bookmarks /.

Chapter Four

Grace In The Face of God

M eet Hannah. Her name means "grace." Like Zlelponi, she lived in the period of the Judges, maybe 40 years later. Also, like Zlelponi, she was barren when God found her.

The similarities pretty much end there. Hannah's husband, we are told, loved her. But the even bigger difference is unlike Zlelponi, Hannah goes regularly to the Tent of Meeting in Shiloh to worship God. She was remarkably dependent on God and longed to experience His heavenly favor over and over again.

> *"There was a certain man from Ramathaim...He had two wives; one was called Hannah and the other Peninnah. Peninnah had children, but Hannah had none. Year after year this man went up from his town to worship and sacrifice to the LORD Almighty at Shiloh...Whenever the day came for Elkanah to sacrifice, he would give portions of the meat to his wife Peninnah and to all her sons and daughters. But to Hannah he gave a double portion because he loved her, and the LORD had closed her womb." (1 Sam 1:1-5)*

OK, we must lay aside our cultural understanding of what love looks like as we enter the narrative. My wife would not leap for joy if I just gave her more meat to express my love for her. My wife would have already been upset when I brought wife #2 into the household. No judgment from me.

But the storyteller is informing us that Elkanah really did love Hannah and showed it in culturally approved ways. It would seem he loved her even more than he loved his second wife and his children with her. It gets complicated. And yet, that nasty, critical voice in Hannah's head wouldn't let her experience that love. Maybe she is even questioning it.

Brené Brown says "Shame is that gremlin who says...you are never good enough and who do you think you are."[1]

Ironically, "Grace" is riddled with shame. We all get it. "Shame strikes at our basic sense of worth, making us feel that we are fundamentally 'wrong' or not good enough. Shame becomes part of our global self-schema and becomes a lens through which all experience is filtered."[2]

One person rightly says, "Shame feels like a solitary pain...But in fact, shame in all its forms is relational. Shame is the experience of self-in-relation when 'in relation' is ruptured or disconnected. A chronic sense of self-in-disconnection becomes a profound sense of isolation which in turn leads to feelings of despair and unworthiness."[3]

This is where God finds Hannah—but He will not leave her there.

Did I mention Penninah, the second wife's name, means "Beautiful Flowing Hair?" Ouch. Did I mention Beautiful Flowing Hair had children (plural)? Double ouch. And further, did I mention Penninah endlessly tormented Hannah, shoving her barrenness in her face again and again?

> "Because the LORD had closed her womb, her rival (Hebrew-tzarah) kept provoking (Hebrew-ka'as) her in order to irritate (Hebrew-ra'am) her. This went on year after year. Whenever Hannah went up to the house of the LORD, her rival provoked (Hebrew-ka'as) her till she wept and would not eat." (1 Sam 1:6-7)

The word for rival is *tzarah* in Hebrew. It means "adversary" in Psalms, but in common parlance, it was the generic term first wives used to refer to the often challenging second wife. It implies an ongoing war for their mutual husband's favor and attention. Such was Hannah's problem.

"Beautiful Flowing Hair" missed no opportunity to provoke (Hebrew-*ka'as*) Hannah. She was a constant irritant, driving poor Hannah to distress and, in fact, humiliating and shaming (Hebrew- *ra'am*) her as much as she possibly could. I love how the author portrays Hannah as a real, three-dimensional human being. Anyone could relate to her.

You may ask, "Couldn't Hannah just be reasonable and *choose* to believe Elkanah really did love her and honor her as she was?" Really? How do you think that would have gone? Terribly.

It's brain science. The prefrontal cortex, that part of our rational brain that chooses, weighs pros and cons, and is reasonable and able to make accurate judgments based upon evidence, is also the weakest part of our brain, particularly when under duress.

It is then that our emotional brain naturally takes over. It is how we are designed. You've heard of chemicals and hormones that kick our brain into action at almost light speed, like dopamine, oxytocin, and cortisol—very powerful chemicals that are released when triggered by stress, such as when a relational competitor steals our spouse's devotion and attention—or we are afraid that has happened. Those chemicals immediately shut down our prefrontal cortex. When we are attacked by a bear, we don't want to take time to gather data, weigh options, consider long-term consequences, and then act. No, we want an immediate fight, flight, or freeze.

So, forget bears. What happens when, right in front of you, Beautiful Flowing Hair leans in and whispers sweet nothings into your husband's ear? Boom. Automatic fight, flight, or freeze. It is subconscious and happens at light speed. Grace gives way to reactionary behavior. What can Hannah do? Very little.

This does not make Hannah a bad person, a weak, or a broken person. It means she is human. To be clear, there are no muscle groups to manage your emotional midbrain. Its workings are largely unconscious and automatic. So, trying harder to be "grace" is not going to work well. It could be said that your brain has a mind of its own. She can't just will away the shame in her brain. She can't just demand her critical inner voice to shut up. It is destructive and mean by nature. It is against you participating in the dance. It says, "Not so fast!

You are just not that lovable. Your husband may say he loves you, but you are a disappointment."

As one blogger says,[4]

> "[That] critical inner voice reminds us constantly that we aren't good enough and don't deserve anything good. It tends to be louder and meaner in some of us than others, and it tends to pick on us more or less at different points in our lives. Yet, one thing's for sure. As long as we are listening to this dangerous critic that twists our reality, we cannot really trust our own perceptions of what others think of us. To one degree or another we are lonely and feel broken."

We can label that critical inner voice as, the beast, shame, or fear, but we all have it—maybe a little, maybe a lot. It is not reasonable. It does not respond to our reason or anything else we may choose to do.

So, I am NOT going to tell Hannah she should just try harder to be gracious or choose to forgive her rival. It will not work. It's a brain thing. Would you agree? What has your experience been?

No guilt trips or shaming here. That would be counterproductive.

So, Elkanah can give her a double portion of the offering, a public symbolic declaration that he loves her more than Peninnah (1 Samuel 1:5), and it still does not have the power to change how Hannah feels. She can choose to believe she is Wife #1 in good standing until the cows come home. She can argue to herself that Elkanah's love isn't a function of how many children she has or doesn't have. But...

How do you think this went inside Hannah's brain?

OK, let me ask the obvious question here. If her husband really loved her, why did he marry another wife? The rabbis speculate that it was done because Hannah was childless.[5] Culturally, Elkanah wanted children, particularly a boy who would inherit his wealth. They added that Hannah likely would have agreed with the plan—to a certain point. Perhaps she suggested it, like Sarah and Rebekah before her. It worked out so well for them, right? No, not really.

I think we can now see that this only made her shame worse. The abundantly fertile second wife became the functioning first wife. She is bearing him all-important children. That is what Hannah's critical inner voice is no doubt telling her 24/7, and there is little she can do about it.

In the last chapter, I mentioned the amazing book *The Joy Luck Club* by Amy Tan. It is about four Chinese American matriarchs who struggle for worth in the misogynistic culture of mid-20th-century China.

An-Mei was the daughter of a woman who had become the fourth wife of a wealthy Chinese businessman (the third concubine). We are told her first husband passed away, and for economic reasons—not love—she agreed to be this man's fourth wife. So, in that Chinese culture, she sold out her *value* as the first wife to gain security for herself and her daughter. She took on the huge societal shame of being a concubine—and worse, she became the third concubine, regularly mistreated, and diminished by three women ahead of her in the worth pyramid. What was she to do? In her culture, you learned to be quiet and accept your diminishment, no matter how badly your husband and the other "more worthy" women treated you.

In her terminology, she swallowed her shame and sadness.

But it turns out that shame, by nature, refuses to be swallowed. It lingers. It burns. It erupts. It affects all aspects of your life. In the end, An-Mei's mother succumbed to the shame and took her own life. What is the moral of the story for An-Mei?

"On that day I learned to shout...I tell you the story because I was raised the Chinese way. I was taught to desire nothing, to swallow other people's misery and to eat my own bitterness...My mother did not know her worth until it was too late...[its] too late for her but not for me."

If there were no God, or if there were no God who willingly bends low to raise up the devalued—those who the culture determines have no worth—the unloved, and unlovable—no one who has their backs—then I would be a fan of just crying out to the empty heavens.

But there is such a God. Fortunately, Hannah knew it.

Here's where Hannah becomes a true hero of the faith and, rightly, should take her place in the hallowed hall of daughters of the Most High. This may sound strange to you at first blush.

Why? You may have been taught true women of faith swallow their shame and injustices. You might have been told a true woman of faith wouldn't let all her rival's shenanigans affect her. She would just choose to be secure and find her value and worth in the eyes of her husband and in God, despite how she feels. She would choose to forgive Peninnah and somehow choose joy. Whatever that means.

Maybe you would expect Hannah, being "Grace," to write some praise song on the goodness of God. Maybe that would move God to finally bless her. If that is what you have been told, I have one question for you. How's all of that going for you?

No! God forbid. Hannah is cut from a very different cloth. She seems to have learned her well-being, her sense of worth, her favorability, and even her very identity come first and foremost from the measuring gaze of God, *lipnay Elohim*.

Look at the *Spirit-Sourced Fruit* spectrum again.

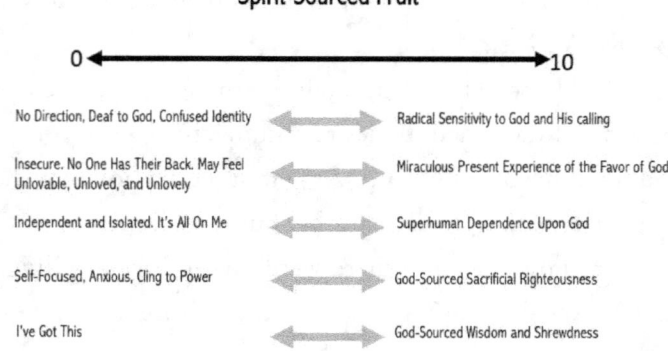

Spirit-Sourced Fruit

0 ←——————————————————→ 10

No Direction, Deaf to God, Confused Identity	Radical Sensitivity to God and His calling
Insecure. No One Has Their Back. May Feel Unlovable, Unloved, and Unlovely	Miraculous Present Experience of the Favor of God
Independent and Isolated. It's All On Me	Superhuman Dependence Upon God
Self-Focused, Anxious, Cling to Power	God-Sourced Sacrificial Righteousness
I've Got This	God-Sourced Wisdom and Shrewdness

I believe that upon inspection we can begin to see the Spirit's fruit of a "miraculous present experience of the favor of God" and a "superhuman dependence upon God." Hannah seems to know how dependent she is on God to experience the sense of favor and favorability that she is missing. It is very sophisticated. Is it me, or does she just seem to know she will not get that higher sense of needed favor from her husband, no matter how much meat he lays on her plate? She seems to know she can't make her brain feel lovable, loved, or lovely. She can't change her barrenness, to be sure. Such transparency, such vulnerability.

But she can go to Shiloh, to the Tabernacle of God, and look up into the face of God, *lipnay Elohim,* and cry out to the One who loves her as she is. Not just once. This was her practice.

> *"This went on year after year. Whenever Hannah went up to the house of the LORD, her rival provoked her till she wept and would not eat. Elkanah her husband would say to her, "Hannah, why are you weeping? Why don't you eat? Why are you downhearted? Don't I mean more to you than ten sons?" (1Sam 1:7-8)*

A couple of things. First, bless his heart. To his credit, her husband at least notices her emotional pain and asks her why she is crying. Even though it seems Elkanah didn't intervene much in the relational fighting between his wives, I do imagine this being sincere. You may disagree.

Secondly, even I can hear Elkanah's words as serious mansplaining. I do believe he is well-meaning, but it feels like gaslighting to shift it to be about his problems versus hers.

Third, Elkanah says something dangerous yet very insightful to her. "Why are you downhearted?"

Literally, "Why is your heart bad?" Whether this was well received or not by Hannah—I wouldn't like it—but I am so glad he said it. Why? Even 3,000 years later, I can relate to Hannah. She is so very human.

Of course, her heart is bad, beat up, enraged, wanting vengeance, retribution, and justice—wanting a rescuer, someone who has her back, some relationship that removes her shame, her helplessness, and her disgrace. I would too. Too often we believe good Christians can't feel those feelings. Hannah did. I do too.

Aren't you tired of whitewashed, smiley-masked biblical characters? I am.

In contrast to the Israel of the Judges, the author places Hannah, the traumatized and beat-up wife who realizes she is so dependent upon God, in the Tent of Meeting at Shiloh. Unlike Israel, she cries out to God for a rescue—a rescue that only God can perform.

Praise the Lord. Her cries are not pristine or theologically clean. She is crying out with a *bad heart* and an embittered soul (1 Samuel 1:10). Let's hear this. God receives such as this into His arms. God loves needy, abused, lonely, shamed, and embittered real people. He rescues them and loves them until they feel loved and worthy again.

Don't misunderstand what I am saying. What sets Hannah apart as one of the great women of faith in the Bible is this: Even though she is wounded, even though she likely *hates* Beautiful Flowing Hair a little or a lot, her faith drives her to take her *bad heart* into the *lipnay Elohim* presence of God. She is experiencing a superhuman dependence on God.

> *"[Hannah] was deeply distressed and prayed (Hebrew-palal) to the LORD and wept bitterly. And she vowed a vow and said, 'O LORD of hosts, if you will indeed look on the affliction of your servant and remember me and not forget your servant, but will give to your servant a son, then I will give him to the LORD all the days of his life, and no razor shall touch his head.' As she continued praying (Hebrew-palal) before the LORD (Hebrew-lipnay Yahweh), Eli observed her mouth." (1 Sam 1:10-12)*

In 1 Samuel 1:10 and 12, we are told she is praying to the Lord. The Hebrew word *palal* is intense and has a technical meaning. She is emphatically bringing a specific request to the only one with the authority and capacity to fulfill her wish.

There is another sense to the word *palal*. It can mean "to fall." She has likely fallen to the ground on her face. How different this is from both Chill and Zlelponi.

She is poignantly aware she is in the very presence of the Creator God who is *for* her. This is another trait of ideal biblical womanhood. In verse 12, she is described as entreating God, *lipnay Yahweh*.

She has left nothing to chance. She gets as close as she can to the Judge who alone can give her the desire of her heart. She is praying right up in God's face, *lipnay Yahweh*. She would see the Lord's gaze upon her and her pain. She would have God see deep into her soul. She came—as she was—into the penetrating gaze of God—as God is.

What does the Spirit-empowered biblical woman do in the raging swirl of such injustices? She goes to her savior, God, to make a formal complaint. She cries out to God. She refuses to fake it till she makes it. She doesn't need a counselor; she doesn't need more meat—she needs to feel favored and favorable again. She needs a rescuer.

Hannah is so unique. She has that powerful, God-sourced sense that He has her back despite her circumstances. Despite how she feels, she puts herself in a dependent posture before the Lord.

This biblical dependence is <u>God-initiated,</u> intentional, and a free reliance upon the capacity of another. It is the willing giving up of illusions of control that carries no element of subordination or subjugation. It has no connotation of being right or wrong, or doing right or not doing wrong. No grades, no judgment, no shaming, no weakness. Rather, it is an act of choice by a free agent.

This God-sourced trait is greater than the power of her critical inner voice, which just might accuse God of being the one who closed her womb in the first place (1:6), maybe as a punishment for some unknown sin or indiscretion.

That is why this dependence must be God-sourced—not birthed from within us somehow. We can't just try harder to be dependent. We can't just choose to have such trust. It is not innate to humanity, man, or woman. Dependence is a four-letter word for fallen humanity.

Hannah is one of the best biblical examples of what such dependence looks like in human flesh. People who have this gift from God often go right up to God's face with their complaints. This is not An-Mei's shouting to the sky. Hannah cries out to God, hiding nothing. She does not hide behind some tree in the garden or try to cover her shame behind some flimsy frond like Adam and Eve did.

I liken this to the Lord's table in a way. In my years as a Christian, I have seen communion misunderstood and misused. In the first communion, Jesus required nothing of the disciples before they participated. Did they need to have a cleansing bath, a *mikveh*?[6] No. Did they need to make a viable confession of their sins? No. The table was for them as they were. The table was not dynamic because those who came were righteous. No. The table and the message it told is of a Savior who has come to pursue sinners, embrace the unrighteous, and pay for all the sins and bad-heart stuff that would keep them from experiencing that love. It is for hurting participants.

Come, *lipnay Elohim,* broken-hearted, bullied, sinners, angry, embittered, and diminished, because your healing and redemption are in His eyes. There we cry out in our hurts and pains.

Hannah came, as she was, *bad heart* and all, daring by faith to present her body as a living sacrifice, dedicated and splayed before God's eyes. That is deep, heavenly-sourced faith. That is trust. That is God-initiated dependence.

She didn't wait until she wasn't angry anymore. She came to God angry. No fake smile. No fake anything. She vulnerably confesses to the High Priest Eli that she is deeply troubled (1:5; Hebrew- *qasheh*), filled with great anguish (1:16; Hebrew *-shiach*) and sad with vexation (1:16; Hebrew-*ka'as*). Amazing vulnerability.

Note what she prays for. I will admit that at times, I have prayed *against* my enemies. I am not proud of it. I am also not alone. There are so many Psalmists who chose that path (cf., Ps 5:10, 17:13). All I am saying is that I wouldn't blame her if she prayed at least for a bad hair day for Peninnah. Do you know what I mean?

But the desire of her heart was that God would give her a son. In return for that gift, she promises to give the child to the Lord. In that day, all firstborn sons are God's. If parents did nothing, the boy would enter full-time service of God at the Tent of Meeting when old enough. Optionally, parents could "redeem" their firstborn son by making a specific burnt offering at the Tent of Meeting. Hannah commits her son to the Lord for holy service. She will offer no redemption offering. He will not be the son who receives Elkanah's inheritance. That would go to Beautiful Flowing Hair's firstborn, I suppose. Hannah's son will be Lord-bound for all his days.

Check this out. As she is praying, face to the ground, *lipnay Yahweh*, something happens to Hannah. Grace experiences grace (1:18- Hebrew- *hen*). She experiences the God who has not forgotten her, the One who still has her back.

How do we know? The bitterness and anguish of her heart are miraculously removed (1 Samuel 1:18). We have to assume that the successful operation was conducted by the very hands of God. She ends her fasting, and we are told her face is "no longer to her"—meaning she is no longer the same person she was when she entered *lipnay Elohim*.

There have been times when I have experienced such a powerful surgery. There was one particular church leader's meeting where I felt unjustly treated, dishonored, and disrespected. When I came home, emotionally bruised, and depressed, I took my Bible to the streets. It was dark, fortunately, so there were only a few witnesses. I walked up and down the neighborhood, repeating Psalm 88 aloud to God.

> *"May my prayer come before you [God]; turn your ear to my cry. For my soul is full of trouble and my life draws near the grave... You have put me in the lowest pit, in the darkest depths. Your wrath lies heavily upon me; you have overwhelmed me with all your waves. Selah. You have taken from me my closest friends and have made me repulsive to them. I am confined and cannot escape; my eyes are dim with grief. I call to you, O LORD, every day; I spread out my hands to you." (Ps 88:3-9)*

Over and over, I would cry out these accusing words to God with my Bible awkwardly lit up by a tiny flashlight, trying not to trip on anything on the dark sidewalk. In my anger and tears, my voice would ramp up when I got to the end, particularly the very last phrase of the Psalm.

"Your wrath has swept over me; your terrors have destroyed me. All day long they surround me like a flood; they have completely engulfed me. You have taken my companions and loved ones from me; the darkness is my closest friend." (Ps 88:16-18)

Yeah. I had a bad heart, to be sure, but miraculously, I knew where I could find healing, favor, and justice. It worked, but admittedly, it took a very long time. Like Hannah, I suppose, I too finally felt "my face was no longer to me." Relationships still needed to be addressed, to be sure. But at that moment, I didn't need the favor of others as much as I was content to depend upon God's favor for me.

And so, God opens her womb, and Hannah gives birth to the great prophet and king-maker Samuel, meaning "His Name is God."

Contrasting stories

These two women, Hannah and Zlelponi, are both similar and contrasting. In one case, God pursues the woman out of innate love for the unloved. In the other case, the woman pursues God because she somehow, miraculously, believes she has a heavenly benefactor who can give her the sense of favor and favorability she longs for.

Even the names from the two accounts subtly reflect the contrast. Samuel's dad, Elkanah, means "God has created" or "God possesses." Both are statements of God's sovereignty in the story. In contrast, Manoah means "Chill"—stalled—dead in the water. Perhaps it reflects that there is no longer a restlessness in the heart of Israel for a restoration to that lost or forgotten *lipnay Elohim* experience.

In Judges, Zlelponi is described as *barren*. In 1 Samuel, it is recognized that *God has closed Hannah's womb* (1 Samuel 1:6). Similar and yet very telling. In the former, childbearing has human and scientific explanations, maybe fate-borne. In the latter, God is sovereign, responsible, and the arbiter of inequities and injustices.

So, Hannah naturally goes to the court to cry out to the Sovereign Judge for respite. In Zlelponi's case, there is no crying out—no going before the Lord—that is recorded.

May I take a shot at a Hannah-esque prayer for all who feel helpless and unfairly treated today?

"God, I have a bad heart. I can't help but feel small in the eyes of family and friends. I feel bullied, broken, and helpless to do anything about my lot. I am just not enough. It is not fair. This is not just. What have I done to deserve this? I am here, looking up, in desperate need of feeling your favorable measuring gaze. It is not enough for me to know you love me and are proud of me. I desperately need to experience it deep in the murky, critical shadows of my head. Now, please. I am here in a dependent posture, *lipnay Elohim*. Where else would I go? No one else has the power to hear my just case and to give me respite. I am here, but I still feel like darkness is my closest friend."

Beloved, I want to encourage you to keep saying the *Simple Uncluttered Gospel*[7] twice a day for 45 days. I need to say it every day as well. Repetition is critical. It is a gospel presentation for that unreached mission field, your critical inner voice. Paul says that the gospel is the power to believe. Believe what? Well, among many things, it is the power to believe that God truly loves you, even though you may currently feel like a second spouse: unlovable, unloved, and unlovely.

We will look at a very unlikely heroine next. Ya'el is one of the few women in the Bible who has a worship victory song about her. Enjoy.

Engage Questions:

1. What did you learn that you did not know before?

2. Hannah is one of the greatest examples of flesh and blood dependence upon God in the entire Bible. Thoughts?

3. Share a time when you prayed with a bad heart, like Hannah *lipnay Yahweh*. Or when such a prayer would have made a real difference—and you wish that you had.

1. B. Brown, "Listening to Shame."

2. Rutledge, "Shame." .

3. DeYoung, "Chronic Shame," 18.

4. PsychAlive, "Nobody Likes Me."

5. Kadari, "Hannah."

6. A Mikveh is a pool of natural water in which one bathes for the restoration of ritual purity.

7. Simple Uncluttered Gospel bookmarks are available at https://gospel-app.com/product/women-simple-uncluttered-gospel-bookmarks /.

Chapter Five

Ya'el: The Beguiling Mother

L et's stay in the time of the judges to visit our next amazing daughter of the
Most High. Remember, it was the time when everyone was doing what
was right in her or his own eyes. The people were following their own desires
and were not serving the Lord. Maybe those are the same, or two ends of a single
spectrum. Not a good time for a woman in the land.[1]

Into this chaos emerges Ya'el, a Kenite—not even an Israelite—who steps up
and takes her place among the great heroines of Israel.

Who is she? Ya'el is the wife of a Kenite tribal leader by the name of Heber,
who was the great-nephew of Moses' wife, Zipporah, whom we will look at in
the next chapter.

> *"Now Heber the Kenite had left the other Kenites, the descendants
> of Hobab, Moses' brother-in-law, and pitched his tent by the great
> tree in Zaanannim near Kedesh" (Judges 4:11).*

Interesting footnote. Hobab can mean either sweet or deceitful, depending
on its context. We will see that as a perfect description of Ya'el as well.

Back to our story. There is a massive battle coming between the great female
judge of Israel Deborah, and the Canaanite King Jabin. Technically, the battle
was fought between their two generals, Barak and Sisera, respectively—but
everyone knew who was in command.

We are told the ruthless Canaanite general Sisera had nine hundred
chariots. That makes him a ridiculously powerful force to be reckoned

with—unbeatable, in fact. To make matters worse, he had a reputation that would make Darth Vader jealous. He was brutal and relentless.

> *"The Israelites cried out to the LORD; for [Sisera] he had nine hundred iron chariots, and he had oppressed Israel ruthlessly for twenty years" (Judges 4:3).*

In stark contrast, the armies of Israel were, to overstate matters, a disunified and ill-equipped bunch of shepherds and fishermen. Everyone doing what was right in their own eyes doesn't serve national defense very well, does it?

Even if a real leader could inspire the disparate Israelite tribes to work together, it still wouldn't have meant much to the alpha predators that ran rampant in the Levant. Israel's military establishment was decades behind the rest in terms of technology. The enemies were well into the Iron Age. Israel was still in the Pitchfork Age. Time and again, better-equipped armies shredded Israel's inadequate and outdated forces.

But this time, largely due to the prophetic charisma of the remarkable lady judge, Deborah, Israeli General Barak was able to gather ten thousand soldiers of Israel—a miracle all on its own. Still, no one would have imagined they would be victorious over nine hundred chariots.

The battle lines were set in the strategic Jezreel Valley. Sisera, with his crack troops and advanced chariots, lined up at the base of the vast valley on the Kishon River. The Israelite General Barak and his ragtag army huddled on the slopes of tiny Mount Tabor.

Deborah had already prophesied an Israeli victory—but even stranger, God told her the battle was to be won by a woman. In fact, she added, the great iron-fisted, invincible Canaanite general Sisera would be handed over to a woman. That would be a matter of great public shame.

I wonder how Barak heard that statement. Was he hurt or offended that he would not get the victory? After all, he was a man.[2] Or likely, he thought Deborah meant she would get the credit. Either way, he seemed ready and willing to play his role in this wild gamble—even if Deborah received all the acclaim. Truth be told, God had another, more unlikely woman in mind.

The Bible records the result of the fierce fighting in only two short verses.

> *"At Barak's advance, the LORD routed Sisera and all his chariots and army by the sword, and Sisera abandoned his chariot and fled on foot. But Barak pursued the chariots and army as far as Harosheth Haggoyim. All the troops of Sisera fell by the sword; not a man was left" (Judges 4:15-16).*

Literally, God threw the Canaanite army into confusion (Hebrew-*hamam*; cf., Ex 14:24, 1Sam 7:10), as only God could do. The shocking result was one of the greatest military victories of Israel—an ill-equipped Israeli army defeated the greatest force ever gathered on the Jezreel Valley. I think it is safe to say only Deborah really believed it could happen.

Now the story gets even more interesting. Sisera's shredded and disheartened troops retreat to the northwestern corner of the Jezreel Valley, only to be slaughtered there. Their larger-than-life ruthless commander, Sisera, had abandoned his command and ran on foot in the other direction to Kedesh, likely an encampment on the western side of the Sea of Galilee.

There he happens upon the "sweet and deceitful" Ya'el.

> *"Sisera, however, fled on foot to the tent of Ya'el, the wife of Heber the Kenite, because there were friendly relations between Jabin king of Hazor and the clan of Heber the Kenite" (Judges 4:17).*

A couple of notes. The Kenites were likely a loosely held confederation of bedouin tribes—largely sheep and goat herders—scattered throughout the Levantine region, from the Arabian Peninsula to the Sea of Galilee. Their home base, if there was such a thing, was likely Arad in the Negev, near the southern tip of the Dead Sea.

They had no grand political aspirations. Their allegiances were as fluid as they could be. At times, some of the tribes aligned with Israel, while others fought against them. Heber, we are told, was part of the Kenites who migrated to Napthali after contracting a treaty with the Canaanite King Jabin.

So, when Sisera stumbled into Heber's encampment, he would have expected to be offered asylum. Heber, his family, and tribe, by the covenant with the Canaanite King Jabin, were allies of Sisera. Perhaps the desperate general was thinking or hoping he had found a safe place where he could rest and be protected until he could head north to the safety of Hazor and King Jabin's great fortification. Maybe he personally knew Heber? We can't be sure. Either way, he would have had high expectations he would be extended hospitality and protection. He was safe now—at last, he could rest.

A word about hospitality. Among Bedouin people, nothing was more important than hospitality. Here are some thoughts by Dr. Clinton Bailey.

> "One side of a Bedouin tent is always wide open, to signify that all guests are welcome. Screening a guest by asking him about his tribal affiliation is frowned upon as uncouth. Bedouin law even stipulates that a guest has the right to remain for three and a third days. In the Bedouin value system, which requires a tent owner to share with strangers what little he has, hospitality enjoys the same prestige as bravery in battle. One popular definition of a man is he who 'strikes with a sword and feeds a guest meat.' Owing to the generosity involved, therefore, a Bedouin derives honor from receiving guests...One poem tells a potential host in a remote place that, upon seeing travelers pass by, he must rise and 'stand in front of the tent till they see you and turn.' ... Once a Bedouin becomes a host, he must seek to make his guest comfortable. On the assumption that guests have been traveling, water is traditionally provided for cleaning and cooling the feet, and drink is offered to quench thirst and revive the guest from fatigue. The host then provides cushions or some improvisation of textiles on which guests can recline with ease; and when a guest enters a tent, the common instruction is to

'elbow in' (*kawwi*), which in Bedouin parlance means to lean on one's elbow, reclining on such a cushion."[3]

This day, Heber is not in camp and so his wife Ya'el is the one to extend hospitality. She does. Ya'el goes out—i.e., "stands in front of the tent"—and bids Sisera to "turn in."

Of course, Sisera accepted her invitation. Why wouldn't he? No one would ever suspect a bedouin, much less a bedouin woman, much less a political ally, would betray the sacrosanct traditions of hospitality.

"Ya'el went out to meet Sisera," as per custom, and said to him, "Come, my lord, come right in. Don't be afraid"—also as per custom. After his long day, shameful defeat, and rush to stay ahead of a regionwide manhunt that was closing in on him, he had at last caught a break.

I imagine in Ya'el, he saw a kind, motherly figure and settled in for some needed rest and food to regain his energy. He would not be able to stay for long.

So, he entered her tent, and she put a covering over him (4:18). The Hebrew word for *covering* is a difficult one to translate. Suggestions for *semikhah* have included a curtain, covering, rug, garment, and blanket. Some rabbis creatively suggested it was a large washing bowl.

"I'm thirsty," Sisera said. *"Please give me some water."*

Ya'el, playing the part of the gracious hostess, went a step further and opened a skin of milk for the general. After he drank his fill, she covered him up to go to sleep. She was being generous and even motherly. He had one more request before this strategic general could at last relax and get some needed rest.

"Stand in the open doorway of the tent," he told her. "If someone comes by and asks you, 'Is anyone here?' say 'No.'" [nobody: Hebrew- 'ayin] (Judges 4:19-20)

She did as he requested. So accommodating. Such a wonderful Bedouin hostess. Right?

But then, the most unlikely thing happened.

"Ya'el, Heber's wife, picked up a tent peg and a hammer and went quietly to him while he lay fast asleep, exhausted. She drove the peg through his temple into the ground, and he died" (Judges 4:21).

Wow, that's unexpected. Thus, the final irony of our story is Sisera, desperately seeking the relative safety of the borders in the far north, was killed by the wife of an ally, whose clan had broken away from the Mosaic alliance, and by a woman at that.

Historically, there are two lenses through which interpreters tend to view this story.

Some have imagined Ya'el as a young, attractive, vibrant woman—think some Hollywood supermodel, who doesn't stop at offering just the typical fare of bedouin hospitality to the general. Some fancifully imagine she has had sex with him a number of times.[4]

"Why would she do that?" asked some of those over-the-top scholars. In that way, she could exhaust him so much that he would offer no resistance when she drove her stake into his head. They also see sexual innuendos in Deborah's victory song related to Ya'el.

"Between her feet he bowed, he fell, he lay. Between her feet he bowed, he fell. Where he bowed, there he fell, destroyed" (Judges 5:24-27).

After all, she was in a tent alone with a man unrelated to her. And so, she used seduction to accomplish a victory against God's enemies.

The other, and far more likely understanding of the text, comes from Deborah's victory song again, where Ya'el's account is juxtaposed with an awkward parallel scene of the ruthless general's mother waiting for his victorious return to her side and worried he is taking too long.

"Through the window peered Sisera's mother; behind the lattice she cried out, 'Why is his chariot so long in coming? Why is the clatter of his chariots delayed?'" (Judges 5:28).

It seems Deborah and the author of Judges would have us see this more as a tale of two contrasting mothers. Instead of imagining Ya'el as a hot Bedouin female in the prime of her sexual maturity, it is better to imagine her as a more mature woman, a mother, perhaps graying, less sexually vibrant, and more exuding maternal compassion. Indeed, Ya'el mothers Sisera, giving him a blanket and milk instead of water, offering the protection a mother might give to her vulnerable child.

If I were to cast Ya'el for a movie production of the tale, I wouldn't consider some supermodel. I imagine more of the "sweet yet shrewd" Iranian actress, Shohreh Aghdashloo, or the talented Palestinian actress, Hiam Abbass.

Is Deborah suggesting Sisera, the great warrior king, commander of over 900 chariots of war, was at heart, a "momma's boy?" Perhaps. It does make for an interesting story.

Here's what I think. The motherly, "shrewd yet deceitful" Ya'el likely did not go looking for trouble or desire to become a savior of Israel that day. She did not plan ahead of time to go against her husband's political alignments and treaties.

Though the Bible does not say, I am going to suggest it was God himself who gave this unlikely champion a seat at the table and gave her this important task. The same Spirit who threw the Canaanite army into a panic, filled Ya'el with the courage to assassinate the enemy leader and the God-sourced wisdom to know just how to do it.

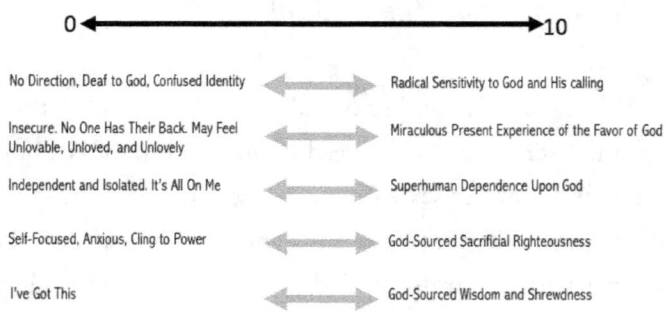

Remember the *Spirit-Sourced Fruit* spectrum? One of the traits we see when women or men are filled with God's Spirit is "God-sourced wisdom and shrewdness." First, they seem to be a little more aware than others that there is an ongoing, often invisible, conflict between God and His enemies, those who seek to destroy God's people. These special women and men seem to be willing to enter the fray, no matter the cost.

In those cases, they seem to reflect God-sourced wisdom, diplomacy, and rhetorical skills to usher shalom into contentious situations—without even firing a shot. But sometimes, as in the case of Ya'el, they will need to use strategic deception. They will lie.

In most ethics classes in Bible colleges today, students are asked about the efforts of Corrie Ten Boom to protect Jews from their Nazi pursuers. Is she following God by lying to the Germans who would surely murder these men and women she has hidden away in her house?

The biblical answer is a clear, "Yes!" It is a war, and the potential costs are high. These ideal women loaded up with God-sourced wisdom seem to get it, sometimes more than their male counterparts.

Biblically, there are times when wisdom—particularly God-sourced wisdom—involves *deception* in order to defeat the enemies of God. In war, there is a place for subterfuge. Of course, one should be very careful. Deception can also be a destructive sin.

But there are times, initiated by God's Spirit when godly participants will be called to use deception. It is risky and dangerous. It could backfire, but often reputations, lives, and futures are on the line. Imagine if Ya'el hadn't killed Sisera.

"But," you ask, "didn't Ya'el sin by murdering a guest?"

No, says the Jewish midrash[5]. Her actions are praiseworthy and even should be considered a *mitzvah*, a religiously commendable act. The rabbis say she acted for the sake of the people of God. "Sin for Heaven's sake is greater than fulfilling a commandment that is not done for Heaven's sake."[6]

Ya'el is not alone in biblical history. Rahab used deception to protect the Israeli spies (Joshua 6). Shiphrah and Puah lied to the great Pharoah's face about the Hebrew mothers (Exodus 1). All are considered great saviors of Israel.

In summary, twenty-four hours earlier, this woman was the respected wife of a tribal leader in league with the enemies of Israel and God. Now, filled with the Spirit of Israel's God, she has become the first operative in the ancient version of Shayetet-13, the Israelite equivalent of Seal Team 6. Why do we suspect she was filled with the Spirit of God here? It is generally understood it was God's Spirit who ordained and empowered the Judges to defeat the enemies of Israel, Othniel (Judges 3:10), Gideon (Judges 6:34), Jepthah (Judges 11:29), the Prophet Judge Deborah, and Samson (Judges 14:6). Though Ya'el was not specifically referred to as a "judge," she is given credit as a judge (Judges 5:24).

Sisera would never have expected what happened. Ya'el would be surprised herself. Though the Bible doesn't explain, some God-thing happened in the heart of Ya'el that changed the trajectory of her life. Wouldn't you have liked to have been there when she explained all of this to Heber?

There was no sign she was rattled, afraid, or intimidated by this massive figure who stumbled into the compound. She seems to know what needs to be done. Like a good mother, she offered comfort to the weary general. Milk instead of water. She offered her blanket to keep him warm. She stood at the open door of the tent to head off any search party.

His very own mother could not have done better or more. He slept in peace, safe and secure in this mother's care. In the beginning, the general would have seen his meeting with this mother figure as a smile from his gods. The Hebrew God had other ideas.

When the Israelite search party finally came by, led personally by Barak,

> *"Ya'el went out to meet him. 'Come,' she said, 'I will show you the man you're looking for.' So, he went in with her, and there lay Sisera with the tent peg through his temple—dead. On that day God subdued Jabin, the Canaanite king, before the Israelites"* (Judges 4:22-23).

In the narrative, there is an inclusio, a repeated phrase that bookends the account. In both Judges 4:18 and 4:22, we read "Ya'el goes out to meet" a man. First, it was Sisera. Afterwards, she goes out to meet Barak.

She had choices. She could have honored her husband's treaty. She could have offered asylum, hoping for a reward. But that was not God's plan. That was not God's calling for this unknown woman.

Instead, God brought the battle to her door. I believe God gave her His Spirit along with the courage and wisdom to accomplish what Barak could not. In fulfillment of the prophecy, Sisera was delivered into the hand of a woman, an unlikely non-combatant, non-Israeli mother in Israel.

Deborah, in the victory song, refers to this unknown Kenite mother as "the most blessed of tent-dwelling women." The Midrashic exposition understands this to refer to the four Hebrew matriarchs, Sarah, Rebekah, Rachel, and Leah. That is great prophetic praise for a non-Jew.[7]

This unlikely, often overlooked, and marvelous woman should definitely be displayed prominently in our grand hall of heroines in Israel. There has never been anyone quite like her.

Will you pray this prayer?

"God, give me such wisdom, Your wisdom, so I can stand up against such powerful foes that would do harm to Your people. The enemy seems better prepared, better equipped, and has infinite numbers. But Your capacity on the battlefield is unequaled, and You stand with me. Give me the shrewdness I need to accomplish my mission and do whatever you desire. I stand ready."

Once again, I want to encourage you to keep saying the *Simple Uncluttered Gospel*[8] twice a day for 45 days. I have personally found repetition is critical. It is a gospel presentation for that unreached mission field, my subconscious yet powerful midbrain. Paul says the gospel is the power to believe. Believe what? Well, among many things, it is the power to believe God truly has your back, even when you find yourself in a position where you feel exposed, ill-equipped, and in danger.

In the next chapter, we will look at another non-Israelite heroine. This woman had to stand up to God Himself.

Engage Questions:

1. What did you learn that you did not know before?

2. What about Ya'el resonated with you?

3. To accomplish her God-given task, she had to use deception. Breaking the sacrosanct, deeply accepted rules and norms surrounding hospitality would have been considered heinous by some. This would have marked her reputation negatively for the rest of her life. Thoughts?

4. Please share any difference that repeating the *Simple Uncluttered Gospel* has made in your life. Use your words and feelings.

---

1. Kadari, "Jael."

2. In a classic "patriarchy", says Terry Real, a member of the senior faculty at the Family Institute of Cambridge and Director of the Gender Relations program at the Meadows Institute in Arizona, "men are supposed to be strong and feel independent, unemotional, logical, and confident. Women are supposed to be expressive, nurturant, weak and dependent." In Caprino, "Patriarchy." In such a culture, men might resist losing authority credit, and power to women. Barak seems different.

3. Bailey, "Hospitality.".

4. Frymer-Kensky, "Jael-Bible."

5. Midrash is ancient Jewish Biblical interpretation and exegesis prominent in the Talmud and other rabbinic literature compiled between 200 and 1000 CE. "Midrash is an interpretive act, seeking the answers to religious questions (both practical and theological) by plumbing the meaning of the words of the Torah. Midrash responds to contemporary problems and crafts new stories, making connections between new Jewish realities and the unchanging biblical text." My Jewish Learning, "Midrash."

6. Kadari, "Yael Wife."

7. Kadari, "Yael Wife."

8. You can get Simple Uncluttered Gospel bookmarks at https://gospel-app.com/product/women-simple-uncluttered-gospel-bookmarks /.

Chapter Six

Zipporah: The Black Woman Who Stood Up To God

H ave you ever felt like you were in the shadow of other men or women? Maybe you felt less educated or not righteous enough, or for whatever reason you had less important things to say than others. Others should do the important strategic work, right? Maybe you married into church "royalty" while your people are spiritually a mixed bag? Maybe you come from a different tribe, socio-economically or racially? You are not alone. You are not the first.

Did you know there was such a woman who stood up to God Himself? About 300 years before Ya'el and the time of the Judges, Moses was traveling to Egypt per God's specific command. On the way, God was about to kill Gershom, the oldest son of Moses and Zipporah. If Moses' wife, Zipporah, hadn't intervened, Gershom would have died. Where was Moses, the great savior of the Hebrews? Good question. It is quite a story!

Zipporah was the Midianite wife of Moses. Her name means "flighty bird," but she was anything but that. Her people were distant descendants of Abraham and his second wife, so not of the line of promise. In the Israelite camp, she was always a foreign woman, and in some quarters, unwelcome and likely subjected to racial slurs. She was never a pure Israelite. And of course, she was married to THE man, Moses.

Why do I bring her up as an important pillar in this Hebrew Women's Hall of Fame? With her quick and decisive action, she will singlehandedly thwart

God's murder of their first-born son, Gershom. Listen to this strange
episode that has confounded scholars for millennia.

> *"At a lodging place on the way, the LORD met [Moses] and*
> *was about to kill him. But Zipporah took a flint knife, cut off*
> *her son's foreskin and touched [Moses'] feet with it. 'Surely*
> *you are a bridegroom of blood to me,' she said. So, the LORD*
> *let him alone. (At that time, she said, "bridegroom of blood,"*
> *referring to circumcision) (Ex 4:24-26).*

Though it is confusing, one thing is certain. Zipporah is the real hero
of the account. Arguably, without her and her intervention, there might
be no Exodus, no promised land, and no fulfillment of the promises of
God to Abraham. It is by her hands that today Israel can celebrate Passover
and Christians can celebrate the Lord's Table. This little-known and poorly
acclaimed heroine of Israel stood up to God Himself. But too few truly
know her story.

Zipporah only appears three or four times in the text: the first time at
the Midian well (Exodus 2), the second time while on the journey to Egypt
(Exodus 4), and finally in the wilderness when Moses met her father Jethro
(Exodus 18). Of her three named appearances in the text, she only speaks
one time, in Exodus 4, and then in a riddle. "Surely you are a bridegroom
of blood to me."

A possible fourth reference to Zipporah happens in Numbers 12, where
Moses' sister Miriam and brother Aaron are "speaking against" Moses and
use what would appear to be a racial slur against Moses' unnamed dark wife.

> *"Miriam and Aaron began to talk against Moses because of his*
> *Cushite wife, for he had married a Cushite" (Num 12:1).*

Could this be Zipporah? Many of us think so. Cush was a tribe of people near
modern Ethiopia. Like the Midianites, they too were dark-skinned. Though I

can't prove it, I suspect Miriam was doing the "Well, they all look alike to me" racial slur so familiar today.

It is also possible Jethro's people could have some Cushite blood. One way or another, we are reminded that even though related to Abraham, Zipporah was likely a denigrated foreign woman in the Israelite camp. Maybe you can relate to her situation.

To be sure, it is a confusing episode.[1] One of the problems in interpreting this particular passage is we have far too many unidentified pronouns. Here is the passage again, with appropriate question marks.

> "At a lodging place on the way, the LORD met him (Moses? Gershom? Eliezer?) and was about to kill him (?). But Zipporah took a flint knife, cut off her son's foreskin and touched his (?) feet with it. "Surely you are a bridegroom of blood to me," she said. So, the LORD let him (?) alone. At that time, she said "bridegroom of blood," referring to circumcision" (Ex 4:24-26).

In a little while, I will make some suggestions so this passage will begin to make more sense. But first, let's set the context. Like so many notables in Israel's history, Moses has a birth account.

> "Now a man of the house of Levi married a Levite woman, and she became pregnant and gave birth to a son. When she saw that he was a fine child, she hid him for three months" (Ex 2:1-2).

In Exodus 2:1, the writer wants to make sure we know Moses, though raised as an Egyptian, is of the tribe of Levi, the later designated *priestly* tribe. How important is this pedigree? He will ultimately take on the priestly assignment of being the one through whom God will communicate the law to His people. He is, by lineage and calling of God, the one who will be used to rescue God's covenant people from slavery in Egypt. To put it another way, he will be God's instrument of redemption for God's firstborn Israel.

Isn't that the Moses we generally have in mind? He is Charlton Heston, bearded and brave, defiantly holding up his staff as the waters of the Red Sea part and the frightened, largely faithless, complaining, and rebellious people skitter across the dry ground like mice scurrying from a bunch of feral cats who are hunting them down.

But that is not the Moses of this text, not completely. He does have those moments. At one point in his younger days, he took the life of an Egyptian who was abusing an Israelite (Ex 2:11-15). But then Moses seemed to emotionally disassemble. Why? The word leaks out that it was Moses who murdered an Egyptian citizen. An angry and offended Pharaoh, the most powerful man in the world, "sought to kill" Moses (Ex 2:15). That will cause anyone distress.

Interestingly, this is a very similar passage to what God will "seek to do" to Moses (i.e., kill, Ex 4:24) on the way back to Egypt. They are sophisticated narrative bookends. On the way to Midian and then back to Egypt from Midian, someone of great power is seeking to kill Moses. The story of his life.

Moses, who was willing at least once to stand up for his people, melts away and runs to a place that couldn't be any more different than his royal upbringing in Egypt.

The Midianites were descendants of one of the six sons born to Abraham and his second wife, Keturah. By the time of Moses' self-exile, they were a confederation of desert tribes, tent-dwelling shepherds scattered from the Israeli Negev to as far south as Aqaba and the eastern shores of the Red Sea in the Arabic peninsula. They were likely aligned with the Cushites of modern Ethiopia.

There he met Jethro, a shepherd of flocks and a priest of Midian. It is difficult to say with any certainty what Jethro's religion might have been, but it would be reasonable to guess it was pretty eclectic, including Baal-peor, Ashtaroth, the Egyptian Hathor, and perhaps even Yahweh[2].

Who is Jethro? He is a larger-than-life character. Historians suggest he seems to have at least six names: "Reuel," "Jether," "Jethro," "Hobab," "Heber," "Keni," and "Putiel." Some suggest the name Jethro was titular, likely meaning "His Excellency," and his birth name was likely Reuel. I would love to read his bio. I am sure he was, in some ways, larger than life.

Back to the story. When we are first introduced to Zipporah, unlike Moses, she has no birth narrative. In fact, she is not even directly mentioned. She enters the stage as one of the seven unnamed, voiceless daughters of Jethro. We can assume she is the oldest non-married or betrothed daughter because she is the one betrothed to this young Egyptian hero.

> *"When Pharaoh heard of this, he tried to kill Moses, but Moses fled from Pharaoh and went to live in Midian, where he sat down by a well. Now a priest of Midian had seven daughters, and they came to draw water and fill the troughs to water their father's flock. Some shepherds came along and drove them away, but Moses got up and came to their rescue and watered their flock. When the girls returned to Reuel their father, he asked them, 'Why have you returned so early today?' They answered, 'An Egyptian rescued us from the shepherds. He even drew water for us and watered the flock.' 'And where is he?' he asked his daughters. 'Why did you leave him? Invite him to have something to eat.' Moses agreed to stay with the man, who gave his daughter Zipporah to Moses in marriage. Zipporah gave birth to a son, and Moses named him Gershom, saying, 'I have become an alien in a foreign land'"* (Ex 2:15-22).

Others have noted there are some similarities between this account and that of Abraham's search for a suitable bride for his son Isaac in Genesis 24. In that account, though, Rebekah plays a prominent role. In this story, Zipporah remains in the background, silent and nameless.

Once again, Moses shows some of his youthful flashes of bravery and willingness to put himself out there for those treated unjustly. For a moment, he sets aside his own navel-gazing and aids the unprotected women against a bunch of shepherds. This is the Moses with whom we are familiar.

As a result of his heroism, he is welcomed into Reuel's clan and given a wife and an unenviable job shepherding his new father-in-law's sheep.

The name he gives his likely first-born son is so telling. Gershom means "stranger here," a glimpse into the emotional state of Moses, I suspect. Imagine a modern Mexican immigrant entering the US's southern border. He finds a home and a job but names his next child "Immigrant Still." This is not a joyful name given by a grateful man who is comfortable in his own skin.

It is a good question to ask at this point, "Who is Moses?" Did he see himself as a descendent of Levi, a descendent of Abraham? A man of Yahweh? Or was he Egyptian? Was he a Midianite of the household of "His Excellency" and heir to the growing sheep empire?

My guess is it is none of the above. I believe Moses was a displaced man, burdened by the trauma of his past—an "immigrant there." I suggest Moses, though he has moments of the right stuff, has deep emotional baggage, particularly related to Egypt and the left-behind Israelite slaves—his abandoned people—who, like him, are still "strangers there."

Forty years pass looking at the back end of aromatic sheep in the hot, unyielding wilderness sun. While there is scholarly debate, it would seem reasonable to imagine by the time eighty-year-old Moses has his audience with a burning bush, his first-born son, Gershom, would be well into his thirties, not an infant or a child.

Then God.

At the burning bush, God does something remarkable. Here is how God later describes His relationship with Moses. "With him I speak face to face, clearly and not in riddles; he sees the form of the LORD" (Num 12:8). Impressive and unique, to be sure. Yet Moses is quite reluctant to accept such an honor. I count five times Moses' questions a direct command of God.

1. "Who am I, that I should go to Pharaoh and bring the Israelites out of Egypt?" (Ex 3:11).

2. "Suppose I go to the Israelites and say to them, 'The God of your fathers has sent me to you,' and they ask me, 'What is his name?' Then what shall I tell them?" (Ex 3:13).

3. "What if they do not believe me or listen to me and say, 'The LORD did not appear to you'?" (Ex 4:1).

4. "O Lord, I have never been eloquent, neither in the past nor since you have spoken to your servant. I am slow of speech and tongue" (Ex 4:10).

5. "O Lord, please send someone else to do it" (Ex 4:13).

To put this in context, the reluctant Judge Gideon questions the validity of the Angel of the Lord only three times (Judges 6:11-22). The murderer Cain dismisses God's entreaties only once (Gen 4:9). Mary, the mother of Jesus, also respectfully questions God only once. Moses? Five times, he tries to turn down God's call.

Is it cowardice? Not likely; we have seen Moses' courage. Is it shame? Is it unbelief? Perhaps. I suggest it is a lack of trust. There is no reason to think Moses had any relationship at all with Yahweh before this episode. Why should he trust this unfamiliar bush god and put himself in such great danger again?

I also think the command of God that he return to the place of his greatest shame triggered a subconscious fear cycle. We all get it. When we are attacked or something happens that threatens our well-being and safety, our brain's amygdala triggers the release of the hormone cortisol, which launches us at light speed into a fear cycle (fight, flight, freeze). It is autonomic and subconscious.

Moses' brain seems to go with "flight." I am not suggesting cowardice. We have seen Moses do some heroic acts that put him in harm's way. No, I think the trigger had something to do with emotions related to Pharoah or Egypt or with his failure to rescue his harshly oppressed people.

Cortisol does what it does in the brain. Neuroscientifically, it immediately shuts down one's prefrontal cortex, that place where you are reasonable and can consider the long-term consequences of words and choices. My point is Moses was probably not thinking straight. It was not all his fault, but it might explain his disrespect to the God of Abraham. In contrast, God showed remarkable, infinite patience with this emotionally traumatized man.

Let me translate Moses' thoughts.

"God, you've got the wrong guy. I can't do this. Me, the savior of the Israelites? Me, stand up to Pharoah? I tried once, and everything unraveled. That's why I am here. I gave up everything that I was, that I owned—my honor, my name, my power, my wealth, my future, my friends, my family—and fled to this armpit of the desert. That is why I shred sandals day after day in this intrepid heat. I would be happy to do some other assignment. Do you want me to go and beat up some more shepherds? Just not Egypt. I cannot look the Israelites in the eyes after forty years. There's too much water under the bridge; I just can't go there. Sorry."

Ok, fast-forward. At last, Moses acquiesces, though I would not be surprised if he had dragged his feet for days or weeks until he couldn't postpone this gig any longer.

I get it. He began his time in Midian with one powerful king to fear. Now he has two. Not just the new Pharoah but also Yahweh, this unknown God who will make Moses do his bidding, though he would rather do anything other than go back.

I wonder if he discussed this new God with Reuel (Jethro). What might "His Excellency" have to say about an even greater "His Excellency" arriving in his realm? It appears Moses makes up some lame excuse to get his father-in-law's blessings.

> *"Then Moses went back to Jethro his father-in-law and said to him, 'Let me go back to my own people in Egypt to see if any of them are still alive.' Jethro said, 'Go, and I wish you well.' Now the LORD had said to Moses in Midian, 'Go back to Egypt, for all the men who wanted to kill you are dead.' So, Moses took his wife and sons, put them on a donkey and started back to Egypt. And he took the staff of God in his hand" (Ex 4:18-20.)*

Moses is headed for an awkward family reunion he never wanted, and there he is to command the new Pharaoh of the superpower Egypt to let Yahweh's firstborn son, Israel, go to worship the long-missing "God of the Israelites." The hesitant, traumatized servant of Yahweh heads to Egypt, headlong into his greatest fear, ordered by a God he is unfamiliar with and can't be sure he trusts. Then, at a stop on the way...

This was the time God ordained to clean up some of the covenantal sloppiness that had occurred since Israel had gone to Egypt. Over the next few weeks and months, they will relearn the precepts of the official covenant God made with Abraham. They will learn what it means to be the special firstborn of Yahweh. They will have to be retaught in simple language and imagery what redemption means and how it is to be accomplished. After all, by this time, they are mainly uneducated slaves, arguably more Egyptian than Israelites. Their concept of God has probably been diluted or confused by the very popular Egyptian religion.

They will also have to reinitiate the Hebrew practice of male circumcision. Why? God says so.

Hear God's earlier words to Abraham.

"This is my covenant with you and your descendants after you, the covenant you are to keep: Every male among you shall be circumcised. You are to undergo circumcision, and it will be the sign of the covenant between me and you. For the generations to come every male among you who is eight days old must be circumcised, including those born in your household or bought with money from a foreigner — those who are not your offspring. Whether born in your household or bought with your money, they must be circumcised. My covenant in your flesh is to be an everlasting covenant. Any uncircumcised male, who has not been circumcised in the flesh, will be cut off from his people; he has broken my covenant...On that very day Abraham took his son Ishmael and all those born in his household or bought with his money, every male in his household, and circumcised them, as God told him. Abraham was ninety-nine years old when he was circumcised" (Gen 17:10-24.)

Ironically, those who are not circumcised must be cut off (Hebrew- *ka'ret*[3]). Six hundred forty-five years later, or so, Israel was apparently still circumcising infants. But was it the same operation? Scholars can't be sure.

Even before God commanded Abraham that every male "shall be circumcised," circumcision, the removal of the foreskin of the male penis, was practiced, in some form or another, by various Ancient Near Eastern cultures, including the Egyptians, Ethiopians, the Syrians, and the Phoenicians[4]. In Saqqara, in Ankhmahon's tomb, Visir of the Pharaoh Teti Dynasty (c. 2345 BCE), there is a bas-relief with a representation of circumcision being done to two light-skinned males, likely slaves of a different race.

While there appears to be evidence of Egyptian priests and royals being ritually circumcised, it was their slaves who were universally required to be circumcised to mark them as being owned by the realm.

Arguably, by the time of the Exodus, all Hebrew males over the age of eight days would have been circumcised. Would the Hebrews have circumcised their boys because of the Abrahamic covenant passed down for over six and a half centuries? Or would they have been circumcised to mark them as slaves, objects owned by the Egyptians? We cannot be sure. Maybe both explanations were in play.

Was Moses circumcised? That is an interesting question, and there is a lot of speculation. Isn't it likely he was circumcised as an infant in his mother's, Jochebed's care? He was three months old when she hatched her scheme to save him by floating him down the Nile in a basket—long past the eight-day requirement for Hebrew boys according to the Abrahamic prescription. Pharoah's daughter quickly noticed he was a Hebrew baby. Could that be why?

Perhaps he was circumcised as he entered the royal Egyptian family? Some suggest he would have had to be circumcised to marry Zipporah in the Kenite tradition.

More fancifully, Midrashim lists Moses among seven special people, including Adam and Noah, who were born circumcised.[5] No comment.

We can be pretty sure he was circumcised by the time of our story because God didn't seek to kill Moses, but rather his uncircumcised son, Gershom.

But this is interesting. Some scholars suggest the Egyptian circumcision and the Hebrew circumcision were noticeably different. Check out Joshua 5:2. The wilderness wandering was over. Moses and the entire generation that had left Egypt, who were circumcised (Josh 5:5), had perished. Only Joshua and Caleb were spared. This "Next-Gen" of Hebrews had finally crossed the Jordan and were preparing for their first Passover celebration in the land of promise.

Earlier, God had instructed Moses that no uncircumcised male could participate in the Passover celebration (Ex 12:48). Yet surprisingly we find out none of the males born in the wilderness had been circumcised.

So, the Lord orders Joshua, "Make flint knives and circumcise the Israelites *again*" (Joshua 5:2). "Again?" What does this refer to? Apparently, Joshua knew exactly what God needed him to do.

> *"So, Joshua made flint knives and circumcised the Israelites at Gibeath Haaraloth" (Joshua 5:3).*

Maybe better, "re-circumcised," or "more completely" circumcised?

Side note: There are some very strange and unfortunate names for cities around the globe. Accident, Toad Suck, Hooker, Colon, Intercourse, Ding Dong, and even one city on an island near Wales called Llanfairpwllgwyngyll. Not kidding. Here's another: Gibeah Haaraloth can unfortunately be translated as "hill of foreskins." Now that's distressed real estate.

> *"Then the LORD said to Joshua, 'Today I have rolled away the reproach of Egypt from you.' So, the place has been called Gilgal to this day" (Josh 5:9).*

Gilgal is a play on the word "roll away," referring to the operation where the foreskin is physically "rolled away." Gilgal can be translated as "Roll away, roll away." Try to get that image out of your head.

Some scholars suggest that the "again" in Josh 5:2 implies the Egyptian practice of circumcision was only partial and incomplete compared to the Hebrew practice. Now they had sharper operational utensils available. Here's Bruce Waltke,

"Flint knives, so abundant in Canaan in contrast to Egypt, were probably required because they were associated with the Israelite complete circumcision. Statues of fighting men in Canaan during the third millennium BC show warriors as fully circumcised. Now in the land the Israelites could freely circumcise themselves properly and remove from themselves *the reproach of Egypt*, the incomplete circumcision."[6]

Is there a bigger point? Sure, back then, God ordained physical circumcision to mark his people as His people. Might it have signified something royal or priestly, like in Egypt? Perhaps. It certainly would have referred to the Hebrews being subordinates and servants to Yahweh. But don't think of modern Western slavery practices. This would have been a true honor. Yahweh is now your official protector. Keep this in mind. Not a bad thing at all. Before the Exodus, they were demeaned, mistreated slaves of Pharaoh. This is an infinitely better relationship.

The mysterious meaning behind the practice of physical circumcision was later rolled back (apologies) to include God's redemption of sinners, rebirth, the giving of a new "circumcised heart," physical and spiritual baptism, the coming of the Spirit into the inner-being of the believer, faith, justification, and adoption to sonship. Paul writes,

"In [Christ] you were also circumcised with a circumcision made without hands, in the removal of the body of the flesh by the circumcision of Christ; having been buried with Him in baptism, in which you were also raised up with Him through faith in the working of God, who raised Him from the dead" (Col 2:11-12).

But back in Zipporah's time, it marked the child as being exclusively of Yahweh and under his protection. If you were not circumcised, you would be "cut off" and certainly could not participate in Passover celebrations.

Now we are getting to the stunning role Zipporah is going to play in the upcoming first Passover. I suggest it has largely been overlooked because scholars are so distracted by some very confusing verses. We will not make that error.

Here is what I believe happened. I will attempt to fill in the pronouns of the Exodus 4:24-26 episode.

> *"At a stop on the way to the first Passover, the Lord stopped Moses and began to cut off (ka'rat) Gershom (i.e., kill), the uncircumcised first-born son of Moses. Moses had not obeyed God's command to Abraham and there were consequences. Why now? Well, Moses is on the way to participate in the very first Passover celebration. Everyone knows that no uncircumcised males may participate in the Passover, even the first one, including Moses' family. God justly began to kill the adult Gershom for crimes against the covenant. The great heroic Moses, perhaps frozen in fear, confusion, ignorance, or incapacitated in indecision, did absolutely nothing. He stood silently and watched. Thank God for Zipporah. Flighty Bird took charge. She found a flint knife, quickly circumcised Gershom, and smeared his blood on the young man's feet. Then Zipporah cried out, 'Gershom, you are blood-protected by my actions.' And God let Gershom live."*

Most translations have Zipporah saying to her detached husband, something like, "Surely you are a bridegroom of blood to me." The word for bridegroom can better be translated as "protector."

The rest is history—Passover redemption history.

Here, the unlikely, dark, female, non-Israelite, non-heir to the covenant of Abraham, Zipporah, rises up to confront the Lord Himself and takes on the robe of a patriarch, prophet, and priest.

Spirit-Sourced Fruit

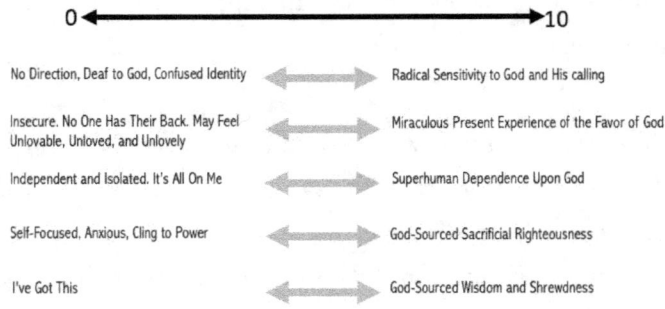

No Direction, Deaf to God, Confused Identity	Radical Sensitivity to God and His calling
Insecure. No One Has Their Back. May Feel Unlovable, Unloved, and Unlovely	Miraculous Present Experience of the Favor of God
Independent and Isolated. It's All On Me	Superhuman Dependence Upon God
Self-Focused, Anxious, Cling to Power	God-Sourced Sacrificial Righteousness
I've Got This	God-Sourced Wisdom and Shrewdness

Unlike Moses, she has no face-to-face instructions from Yahweh. She is Midianite and maybe not even aware of God's covenant with Abraham. She just seems to know what Yahweh desires her to do. I suggest this "radical sensitivity to God and His calling" was a special empowerment of God's Spirit. It has all the earmarks of that gift. Zipporah was not only keenly aware of what God was doing and what she was supposed to do; her awareness was in stark contrast to that of her husband, the "servant of God."

This was her time. She could not sit in the shadows and hope Moses would step up. The life of her son was at stake. Hear the contrasts?

She is decisive. Moses is not.

She is sensitive to what the Lord is doing. He is not.

She is willing to obey. He is reluctant.

There also seems to be a narrative parallel between Zipporah's decisive actions and the instructions to Israel at Passover. Zipporah circumcised Gershom and smeared the blood of the sacrifice on his legs. The Israelites sacrificed a lamb and smeared the blood over the door frame. The results were the same. God's Passover will be celebrated by those circumcised sons according to the covenant of Abraham, which included spouses, daughters, and slaves as well.

Who played the part of the *mohel*[7] of Gershom? Not the mighty Moses. It was Flighty Bird, Zipporah. In so doing, she enters some hallowed Israelite halls.

Abraham circumcised his sons and household. Joshua, we are told, circumcised the Israelites before they entered the promised land. Likely, he gave orders to others, but nevertheless, it was under his authority. Later in Israel's history, it is usually the father, or patriarch, who oversees, commands, or personally does the circumcision.

In a patriarchal world, the story of the Passover is incomplete without a word about Zipporah, the dark foreign woman who like Jacob before her, wrestles with God and overcomes. She seems to understand the importance God places on circumcision and is the only one willing to obey.

She is a great model for modern underestimated daughters of the Most High. It is just another example of God's desire to raise up and honor the disenfranchised and the all-too-often overlooked.

Daughter of the Most High, you were never relegated to be voiceless, a second-class citizen, to dwell in the shadows, or to need others to explain God's desires to you. Your words are not destined to be overlooked footnotes. God would have you listen, speak, and act.

Once again, I want to encourage you to keep saying the *Simple Uncluttered Gospel*[8] twice a day for 45 days. It is a gospel presentation for your powerful midbrain. Paul says the gospel is the power to believe. Believe what? Well, among many things, it is the power to believe God is for you and has your back.

As you say it aloud, take note of how it hits you, what you feel, what emotions bubble up, whether you agree with it or not, whether you have even heard this before or lately.

It's true. The story of Zipporah shows us God can't love you any more if you are "more pure," whatever that means to you. Or whether you have had authority, influence, or voice before. It does not matter to God what your skin color is or what tribe you've come from.

Remember Urie Bronfenbrenner's great quote about children? "Every child needs at least one adult who is irrationally crazy about him or her." So do you, and in Jesus, you have that one person.

Why is it so hard to experience this irrational favor? It's brain science. Nothing has hurt you more than relationships gone sour. God designed your brain to protect you from getting hurt again. It's best to keep expectations low, right? But that is also causing you to subconsciously resist loving and being loved. It may even cause you to avoid paths of honor.

Don't miss what is coming next! Did you know there was a woman who single-handedly saved a major city in Israel? Check it out.

Engage Questions:

1. What did you learn that you didn't know before?

2. It just doesn't matter to God what your skin color is or what tribe you come from. It doesn't seem to matter whether or not you are prepared for the gig (Zipporah or Moses). It doesn't seem to matter whether you are enthusiastic about your calling (Moses) or loved by the people you serve (Zipporah contra Miriam). Push back. Share any "yeah, buts..."

3. What difference has repeating the *Simple Uncluttered Gospel* made in your life? Please be as specific as you can. Use your own words and feelings.

---

1. See Durham, *Exodus*, for an excellent overview. Some suggest that it is God doing the uncircumcised Moses a favor by stopping him before he would be hurt. The thought is that without being circumcised he would have no protection—almost like some talisman that promises protection from dark forces. But it is likely that Moses had already been circumcised in Egypt, either as a child or an adult, or in Midian as a part of a wedding ritual symbolizing that he was of an age appropriate for marriage. Others strangely suggest that it wasn't God at all but a demon.

2. Some suggest that since Jethro was a distant descendent of Abraham, his people would have practiced the Abrahamic covenant of circumcision. I think that it is doubtful. If Jethro was a priest of Yahweh, it would have likely been mentioned.

3. Per Wikipedia, "*Kareth* is the punishment for certain crimes and offences defined under Jewish law (e.g. eating the life blood of a living animal, eating , refusing to be , etc.), a punishment that can only be given at the hand of heaven unto persons of the Jewish faith who are bound to keep the Jewish law, rather than made punishable by any earthly court...By definition, kareth does not apply to non-Jews. Kareth can either mean dying young (before the age of 50 or 60), dying without children, or the soul being spiritually "cut off" from your people after death...Kareth is applicable only when the transgression was done on purpose and without later proper repentance, and is applicable only to Jews." Wikipedia. "Kareth." Wikimedia Foundation. https://en.wikipedia.org/wiki/Kareth.

4. Herodotus, *Antiquities.*

5. See Chabad.org, "Moses." The others include Adam, Seth, Noah, Jacob, Joseph, Moses, and Job.

6. In Wenham, *New Bible Commentary.*

7. A person who performs the Jewish rite of circumcision.

8. You   can   get   Simple   Uncluttered   Gospel   bookmarks   at https://gospel-app.com/product/women-simple-uncluttered-gospel-bookmarks /.

Chapter Seven

The Wise Woman Who Saved a City

T here are great moments in history when one ill-equipped underdog, in a position of weakness or helplessness, must lean on God-sourced wisdom, diplomacy, rhetorical skill, and careful negotiations to save the destruction and death of many. These are the wise peacemakers who don't use guns, tanks, armies, or spears. They use their words to bring peace to many.

In 452 CE, Pope Leo the Great rode out to face the vast, overwhelming forces of Attila the Hun as they bore down on Rome. One man stood in the way of a massive army committed to destroying the powerful See of the Christian Church. Though the conversation was not recorded, Attila turned away and spared Rome.

In 70 CE, as the troops of Rome lay their final siege to the city of Jerusalem, one man dared to plead with the Roman General Vespasian to spare the leaders of the Jewish Sanhedrin and likely save Judaism itself. If Rabboni Johanan Ben Zakkai had not negotiated for the safety of the great scholars of Judaism, at least the school of Hillel, all the theological scholars of Judaism would have surely perished in the destruction of Jerusalem and the Temple.

To accomplish this miracle, Zakkai faked his death by asking his disciples to put him in a closed casket, pretend he had perished, and take him through the gate guarded by Jewish Zealot fanatics who were always on the lookout for traitors who wanted to surrender to Rome. This one heroic man of faith, helpless in stemming the eventual destruction of the Temple of God, was at least able to head off an even larger disaster for Judaism.

Then there was Abigail, the wife of the wealthy yet arrogant and ungrateful Nabal. She brilliantly convinced King David it was a bad idea to take revenge upon her foolish husband and so prevented an unnecessary bloodbath. Her eloquence, diplomacy, and wisdom led the Talmud to identify her as one of the seven female prophets in the Old Testament.[1]

Détente. Political savvy. Statecraft. Such skills have been valued in just about every culture we know. Diplomats were very valued in the often turbulent times of Israel's kings. This tale highlights the work of one largely overlooked and forgotten woman diplomat who hailed from the significant city of Abel Beth Maacha in northern Israel. Sadly, the Bible doesn't even give us her name. Later Jewish midrashim identify her with Serach, the daughter of Asher. Not likely. That would make her well over 400 years old. The point is, among some Jewish scholars, she is legendary.[2]

What cements her place in Midrash's list of twenty-three truly upright and righteous women who came forth in Israel? In her very patriarchal world, this daughter of the Most High single-handedly used only her words and diplomacy to save her great city from certain annihilation.[3]

Was she empowered by God's Spirit for her mission? Though we are not told specifically, like others before her, men and women whom God had raised up to stand strong against His enemies (think Deborah, Gideon, the prophets, David, and Samson), I believe it is highly likely we are to understand she was not alone. Not only was she a diplomat of the ages, but her strength in diplomacy was because she seemed to be empowered with the very wisdom of God.

So, you may or may not be strong, highly educated, or in certain positions of power, influence, and authority, but time and time again in the Bible, the weapons of choice have been words. God-sourced words wrapped thoroughly with God-sourced wisdom soothe anger, stay destruction, and usher in peace.

Context

The kingdom of David had shattered when his third and favorite son, Absalom, raised up an army against him. Still deeply wounded by the betrayal, David was forced to go into exile. After a great civil war, David's vicious General Joab assassinated Absalom and began the politically difficult restoration of

David's throne. Though David was the sole king on the throne, his kingdom was still politically divided north and south between Judah and the rest of Israel. It would be a long and difficult task to restore unity in Israel.

Then this happened.

> *"Now a troublemaker named Sheba son of Bicri, a Benjamite, happened to be there. He sounded the trumpet and shouted, 'We have no share in David, no part in Jesse's son! Every man to his tent, O Israel!' So, all the men of Israel deserted David to follow Sheba son of Bicri. But the men of Judah stayed by their king all the way from the Jordan to Jerusalem"* (2 Sam 20:1-2).

Sheba is described as a useless, good-for-nothing man. Yet he was politically savvy enough to see how the loyalty winds blew. Though hyperbole, the author says in a moment, the fragile unity was shredded. The people of God were once again splintered, with Judah and part of Benjamin to the south and the rest of the tribes of Israel to the north.

Joab pursued Sheba to put an end to this new, very dangerous rebellion. Joab was no stranger to assassinations intended to remove threats to the throne. He had already murdered General Abner against David's wishes shortly after a brokered peace between the house of David and Saul. He chased down and assassinated David's son, Absalom. He then murdered his cousin, Absalom's general, Amasa, in cold blood.

Now this vicious alpha predator was on the hunt for Sheba. Joab had no qualms about violently removing any perceived threats to him or his king. FYI, on his deathbed, David will instruct his son Solomon to have Joab assassinated as well (1 Kings 2:29-34).

One Bible dictionary says this of Joab. He was "a valiant warrior and an able general, and his great influence on public affairs was often exerted for good, as in the rebellion of Absalom and the numbering of Israel...but as a man, he was imperious, revengeful, and unscrupulous."[4] To be sure, he was not a man to be trifled with.

Vengeful Joab and a vast army chased Sheba north.

"Sheba passed through all the tribes of Israel to Abel Beth Maacah and through the entire region of the Berites, who gathered together and followed him." (2 Sam 20:14)

Abel Beth Maacha, or the "Meadow of the House of Maacha," was a prominent city in those days. Tel Abel Beth Maacha is located on the northern border of present-day Israel, just south of the town of Metula and a little west of Tel Dan. Abel Beth Maacha was at the northernmost point of the very fertile Hulah Valley, near one of the four headwaters of the Jordan River. It commanded a crossroads of critical international highways, one led north through the Beqaa Valley, another northeast to Damascus, and even yet another west to the Mediterranean Sea. It, along with nearby Dan, was the northernmost border fortress in Israel. Strategically, it was very important to stop threats from the north.

Apparently, the city of Abel Beth Maacha also had a reputation for diplomacy and détente. Some have speculated it was common for the inhabitants of other cities to bring complicated legal issues to wise arbitrators in Abel for resolution. Their statesmanship was about to be severely tested. Their survival as a city depended upon it.

Abel Beth Maacha served Sheba's purposes well, or so he would have thought. It was a well-fortified town, far enough away from Jerusalem and yet within the boundaries of the northern tribes who weren't officially supporting David yet. He would likely have expected asylum there. He underestimated Joab's stubbornness and one elderly lady's wisdom.

"All the troops with Joab came and besieged Sheba in Abel Beth Maacah. They built a siege ramp up to the city, and it stood against the outer fortifications. While they were battering the wall to bring it down, a wise woman called from the city, 'Listen! Listen! Tell Joab to come here so I can speak to him'" (2 Sam 20:15-16).

Stubborn and relentless, Joab is not going to leave until the job is complete. Though a very brief account, building siege walls takes weeks and months to do, particularly around a city the size of Abel. Notably, the author makes no mention of anyone from the great fortified city of Abel attempting to intervene. There is no record of any city administrator, council, or Levite suing for peace with Joab.

Maybe they tried unsuccessfully. Maybe they were afraid of Joab—for good reason. Maybe they were counting on the other tribes of Israel to rise up and rescue them. But it came to the point in the siege that the city walls were about to be breached. It was not uncommon after a long and arduous siege that the victors would ravage the defeated city and raze her to the ground. This was Joab, after all; his reputation for destruction and revenge was well known.

Then an unlikely, unnamed "wise woman" stood up on the high walls of Abel, on the parapet overlooking the ramp and siege engines that were threatening her city, and she boldly called for General Joab himself to come near the wall for a personal audience with her.

According to one dictionary, *chutzpah* is a Yiddish word meaning "impudence or gall." It is bravery that borders on rudeness. If you have *chutzpah*, you say what you think without worrying about hurting someone's feelings, looking silly, or getting in trouble.

This wise woman was the picture of *chutzpah*.

Here is my expanded interpretive account, faithful to the text.

A wise woman called out from the high walls of the city. "Listen, Listen! Tell Joab to come close; I will speak with him."

Joab went toward her. Then she said, "Are you Joab?" He replied, "I am."

Then she said, "Listen to the words of your handmaid." And Joab said, "I am listening."

I imagine her as an elderly woman who had to be quite well-known in Abel Beth Maacha. No doubt, behind the scenes, the city leaders were trying to determine who would be the one best suited to negotiate with Joab. Being a town with internationally known diplomats and negotiators, there would have been many men to choose from, no doubt. Yet they chose her.

Here's the scene. The feared General Joab stood down on the siege ramp in the hot Israeli sun. Twenty feet above him, looking over the parapet, was an elderly gray-haired Israeli woman who officially requested a private conference with Joab.

She sets the détente stage by, instead of giving her name, calling herself Joab's handmaid. It seems to work. Joab does not appear to feel threatened. She has, in a very short time, done what no one has ever done before. She officially engaged the general in peace talks.

Now what? I love it. She begins with a childlike bromide.

> *"There once was a well-known proverb among the ancient sages,*
> *'Get counsel in Abel. That will settle the matter once and for all'"*
> *(2 Sam 20:18).*

On the surface, it is non-threatening, warm, and maybe even hopeful. This is certainly not how Joab's commanders speak to him. "Let's be wise here." Who could object? I imagine Joab nodding with careful assent. Who doesn't want to be wise? But then Madam Chutzpah lets loose.

> *"I am of Israel, peaceable and reliable. It is you who are seeking to*
> *destroy a city, a mother in Israel. Why do you want to destroy the*
> *Lord's property?" (2 Sam 20:19)*

Remember, we defined *chutzpah* as saying what you think without worrying about hurting someone's feelings, looking silly, or getting in trouble. She indirectly yet publicly accuses Joab of not just wrongly attacking a city but unwisely attacking God Himself.

In Deuteronomy, we read,

> *"When you march up to attack a city, make its people an offer of*
> *peace. If they accept and open their gates, all the people in it shall*
> *be subject to forced labor and shall work for you" (Dt. 20:10-11).*

Joab was a general, not a theologian or a scribe. In his siege planning and preparation, he had failed to consult the Torah—not a surprise. He was a warrior, not a prophet. So now, he had stumbled into very unfamiliar territory, with others watching what he was going to do and say next. He could become defensive, but, hey, she was talking about Torah. He must think.

In a few carefully crafted sentences, the wise woman firmly placed the city of Abel Beth Maacha as the only player in this conflict who was on the side of peace and reason and now on the side of Torah. What can Joab do? Joab was taken aback. Few men or women would ever talk to him this way. Her words seemed to cut him to the quick.

She is indeed one of the greatest daughters of the Most High we have looked at. She did not need an official status, an army, physical strength, or even a name. I believe she had God-sourced wisdom and shrewdness, *chutzpah,* and the skills to bring shalom to a conflict through carefully crafted words and negotiation.

This lady stood up against an army and saved a city. This lady stood on a teetering wall and faced down a renowned murdering warrior who had already assassinated three great generals. This lady stood in the gap for Israel when no man seemed willing. The Bible does not seem surprised that she could accomplish what entire armies could not.

> *"And Joab replied saying, 'Far be it from me! Far be it from me to swallow up or destroy! That is not the case. A man named Sheba, the son of Bicri, from the hill country of Ephraim, has lifted up his hand against the King, against David. Hand over this one man and I'll walk away.'"*

> *"The woman said to Joab, 'His head will be thrown to you from the wall'" (2 Sam 20:20-21).*

Thus ended one of the shortest negotiations for the survival of a town on record. But her story is not yet complete.

Negotiators, in the heat of discussions, often must make commitments, expecting the support of the people for whom they are negotiating. But would the city of Abel follow her lead? Or was she writing checks her bank wouldn't cash? Meaning, would the men of the city, Israelites all, who arguably were pro-Sheba at one point in time, betray her?

> *"Then the woman went to all the people with her wisdom, and they cut off the head of Sheba son of Bicri and threw it to Joab. So, he sounded the trumpet, and his men dispersed from the city, each returning to his home. And Joab went back to the king in Jerusalem" (2 Sam 20:22).*

The author seems to feel no need to shine any additional light on her brilliance as a mother in Abel. It could have been written, "And then she went and did her magic with everyone else in the city, and they followed her in this matter."

Rabbinical writings creatively expand her negotiations with the people of Abel.

> "The woman then went to the people and told them: 'Know that Joab and all Israel are assembled outside the town and seek to kill us, our sons and our daughters.' They asked her: 'And what do they want?' She answered: 'To kill one thousand people. Is it not worthwhile to give a thousand people, to save the entire city from destruction?' They responded: 'Each one will give according to what he has.' She continued: 'Perhaps Joab will go down from the number that he demanded if we mollify him.' She pretended to be on her way to appease him and then returned and told the townspeople: 'Joab has been mollified, and now he wants five hundred people, instead of a thousand. But perhaps if I appease him, he will go down from this number.' So, she went and returned, and said that he had been placated and wanted only a hundred, and then, only ten. Finally, she said to them:

'He only wants one man, who is a lodger [i.e., not from our city].' They asked her: 'And who is he?' She replied: 'Sheba son of Bichri.' The townspeople immediately went and cut off Sheba's son of Bichri's head and gave it to Joab. The threat of war was lifted from the town, and Joab left without harming them."[5]

Is it any wonder then that she joins Deborah, Abigail, and the Prophetess Huldah[6] among the list of twenty-three Israelite women of outstanding righteousness?[7]

She was also raised to a rarified status by Rabbinical writers when they speculate that she was the woman Solomon had in mind as he wrote Proverbs 31.

> "A wife of noble character who can find? She is worth far more than rubies. Her husband has full confidence in her and lacks nothing of value... She is clothed with strength and dignity; she can laugh at the days to come. She speaks with wisdom, and faithful instruction is on her tongue... "Many women do noble things, but you surpass them all." Charm is deceptive, and beauty is fleeting; but a woman who fears the LORD is to be praised. Give her the reward she has earned, and let her works bring her praise at the city gate." (Prov 31:10-31).

The Rabbinical writers go even further to say her story is the unspoken background of Ecclesiastes 9:18. "Wisdom is better than weapons of war, but one sinner destroys much good." If so, I think the author missed his or her opportunity. Wisdom in the mouths of daughters of the Most High is better than entire armies.

I can't think of another time in my lifetime when true shalom-producing chutzpah is in such desperate need on the world stage. The goal of such God-sourced wisdom and détente is not to gain position, power, or name. It is not meant to win elections.

Did the wise woman win? Not in one sense of the word, where one person wins and another loses.

Joab accomplished his goal and ended a dangerous threat to the restoration of David's monarchy. Abel Beth Maacha survived. It's a win-win.

There is another side to the resolution that is worth looking at. The feared, unchallengeable Joab had publicly met his match, a Spirit-filled woman of Israel. Remember, Israel was a very patriarchal culture. This could leave a mark.

Also, Abel Beth Maacha's reputation wasn't unscarred either. Abel was the "mother of Israel," a great and influential fortification of the northern coalition of rebel tribes. In some, maybe many, quarters of Israel, the assassination of Sheba would have been seen as traitorous.

Also, remember the story of Ya'el? The traditions surrounding hospitality and asylum were sacrosanct. For the city to not uphold protection and security for a visitor was unrighteous and considered an offense to the Lord.

What the wise woman accomplished was a greater peace that stopped the imminent slaughter of innocence. It was imperfect, to be sure, yet it brought functional peace to deeply divided, conflicting parties. It brought a moment of rest to the children of Abraham. The greater good was served, and a single wise woman made the difference.

I suspect many women reading this account are also as gifted as the wise woman of Abel Beth Maacha. It is a very special gift and calling of God.

The danger is coming to believe your gifting is ineffective compared to Joab's approach. But that's not true, is it? Maybe it is time to climb to the creaky parapet and start calling out the Joabs of the world. The world will praise you at the city gates.

I want to encourage you again to keep saying the *Simple Uncluttered Gospel*[8] twice a day for 45 days. It is a gospel presentation for your brain. Paul says the gospel is the power to believe. Believe what? Well, among many things, it is the power to believe God is for you and has your back.

As you say it aloud, take note of how it hits you, what you feel, what emotions bubble up, whether you agree with it or not, whether you have even heard this before or lately.

Did you know there was an unlikely woman who stood up in the face of great evil to rescue the lone remaining male heir of King David? Her story could be the screenplay for the next Mission Impossible thriller. Check it out in the next chapter.

Engage Questions:

1. What did you learn that you didn't know before?

2. What can we learn from this wise woman's account?

3. Please share any difference that saying the *Simple Uncluttered Gospel* has made in your life. Use your own words and feelings.

---

1. Adelman, "Abigail.". We will see Abigail again in *Dance, Daughters of the Most High* Volume 2.

2. Kedari, "Wise Woman."

3. Kedari, "Wise Woman."

4. Rand, "Joab."

5. In Kadari, "Wise Woman."

6. We will look at this wonderful character in *Dance, Daughters of the Most High! Vol 2.*

7. In Kadari, "Wise Woman."

Chapter Eight

Jehosheba: The Woman Who Rescued Jesus

T he last amazing Daughter of the Most High for this first book is one of the most overlooked, underappreciated, and, in the grand scheme of things, one of the most important characters in the Bible, male or female. She exhibits one of the most critical of all ideal biblical traits, *righteousness*.

Did you know the line of David was almost completely annihilated at one point in Israelite history? How could that even come close to happening? God said David's line would never end. The Lord promises David, in no uncertain terms, that his line is eternal.

> *"The Lord declares to you that the Lord himself will establish a house for you: When your days are over and you rest with your ancestors, I will raise up your offspring to succeed you, your own flesh and blood, and I will establish his kingdom. He is the one who will build a house for my Name, and I will establish the throne of his kingdom forever…Your house and your kingdom will endure forever before me; your throne will be established forever" (2 Sam 7:11-16).*

Why is this important to us? Jesus was the fulfillment of that prophecy. He was the prophesied seed of David. No line of David, no Jesus. No Jesus and everything would be turned on its head.

In 842 BCE, except for the fast, risky, and deliberate actions of one righteous woman, the last lone survivor of David's line would have been assassinated.

The tales of rulers cleaning the royal house of potential heirs are as old as the hills. Roman Emperor Julius Caesar was assassinated, but the assassins did not kill his great-nephew, Octavius, who succeeded him as Emperor Augustus. The French Revolutionaries made sure to take out the entire ruling family of King Louis XVI of France. Similarly, the Bolsheviks assassinated Tsar Nicholas II of Russia and the entire royal family. No heirs could survive. Puyi, the last Emperor of China, had no heir to the throne, and he wasn't assassinated. Rather, he was forced into an intense and systematic re-education program (i.e., brainwashed) by the Communists until he became a fervent believer in the communist system. The result was the same.

It is also a very common and popular theme for books and movies, such as *The Black Panther*, *The Lion King*, Alexandre Dumas' *The Man in the Iron Mask*, and just about any historic movie about the British monarchy.

Jehosheba's story reads like a Netflix adventure movie. Here's the voiceover for the trailer.

"The stakes are high. Evil has taken over the throne and now rules the land, bent on the destruction of God and the prophecies. There is no hope. Until…God raises up an unlikely champion, a heroic woman of righteousness who will risk it all to save Judah's last single hope."

For historical context, only four generations removed from David, the thrones of Israel and Judah were deeply infected by idolatry and infidelity to God. It can happen so quickly.

Jehoshaphat was David's great, great, great-grandson, the fourth king of Judah. He is described as a good king. He walked in the footsteps of his ancestor, David. Unfortunately, he made one very big and consequential mistake. For the sake of supposed détente between the countries of Judah and Israel, he arranged a horrible political marriage between his son, Prince Jehoram, and Princess Athaliah, the daughter of the vile Israeli royal couple Ahab and Jezebel.

When Jehoshaphat died, Jehoram, likely influenced by his wife, brutally assassinated his six younger brothers to secure his throne. The Chronicler reports that, unlike his father, Jehoram had "forsaken the Lord" (2Chr 21:10). There was little mourning over his death. He was buried in disgrace "in the City of David, but not in the tombs of the kings" (2 Chr 21:20).

He was survived by his only son, the lone legitimate male heir of David, the short-lived and tragic Ahaziah. Ahaziah was only 22 years old when he began to reign and was a political shill for his controlling mother, Athaliah. He was assassinated only one year later.

It was now 841 BCE. The vile Queen, Mother Athaliah, viciously seized the Judean throne for herself and became the undisputed monarch.

How bad was she? Remember, she was likely the granddaughter of the Israelite King Omri—"Omri did evil in the eyes of the LORD and sinned more than all those before him" (1 Ki. 16:25)—and the daughter of King Ahab— "Ahab son of Omri did more evil in the eyes of the LORD than any of those before him" (1 Ki. 16:30)—and Jezebel— "There was never a man like Ahab, who sold himself to do evil in the eyes of the LORD, urged on by Jezebel his wife" (1 Ki. 21:25). If it were possible, she was more black-hearted than all of them put together.

What am I suggesting? If Darth Vader and Disney's Cruella De Vil hooked up and birthed a daughter, she might have Athaliah's pedigree. Based on the text, it appears she has legitimate sociopathic and paranoid tendencies. She was not one to be trifled with.

Her first action was to dispatch (i.e., assassinate) any perceived potential, present, future, or imagined threat to her throne. In her sights was Ahaziah's sole surviving son, the infant Jo'ash, the last living male descendent of David, the last seed of David's official bloodline.

In the middle of this bloody rampage, God raised up Jo'ash's paternal aunt, Princess Jehosheba. Jehosheba means "Yahweh is fullness, happiness."

In one of the greatest stories of palace intrigue ever, Jehosheba, the sister of the recently assassinated King Ahaziah, snuck into the royal chambers, right under the nose of the queen, and kidnapped the royal infant and his wet nurse. I imagine she pulled this off with only moments to spare before the bloody queen could kill the child. Here is how the author of Kings describes it:

"When Athaliah the mother of Ahaziah saw that her son was dead, she proceeded to destroy the whole royal family. But Jehosheba, the daughter of King Jehoram and sister of Ahaziah, took Jo'ash son of Ahaziah and stole him away from among the royal princes, who were about to be murdered. She put him and his nurse in a bedroom to hide him from Athaliah; so, he was not killed. He remained hidden with his nurse at the temple of the LORD for six years while Athaliah ruled the land." (2 Kings 11:1-3)

2 Chronicles 22:11 says she stole (Hebrew: *ganav*) him away by concealing him and his wet nurse in a safe, dark bedroom, a secret chamber, or what we might refer to as a safe room where the Queen wouldn't think of looking.

Now what? How do you keep an infant hidden? They can cry at the least opportune moment. They need special care and food. Certainly, the asylum seekers would be found out and murdered if they stayed in the palace. What could she do? Where could she go? The queen had so many servants at her disposal, no doubt all afraid of her. How long would it be until someone betrayed the infant prince and Jehosheba?

Enter Jehosheba's husband, the chief priest, Jehoiada. Together, they hatched a plot to move the Davidic heir to the Temple complex, just a short walk up a few steps from the Royal Palace and the paranoid Athaliah.

If it were me, I would do it at night when Athaliah was celebrating her good fortune or when her attention was directed elsewhere. It had to be done so no one else knew. No witnesses. It is said that palace walls have ears. No one loyal to the Queen could witness this next step in the rescue.

Once out of the palace, they had to make it to the temple complex without being recognized. You wouldn't want to go into the very public Double Gates at the southern end, the ones nearest the palace. Too many things could go wrong, and too many guards might recognize the infant prince. There were other gates, like the Susa on the eastern wall, the Sheep gate at the north, and the West gate. I wouldn't be surprised if there were hidden tunnels somewhere on the platform that could be used for this clandestine mission. Certainly, Jehoiada would know of the options. Unfortunately, the text does not answer the question of how they transported the child to the temple, but, according to rabbinical writings, Jo'ash was hidden in one of the secret chambers behind the Holy of Holies. Others suggest he lived secretly in one of the upper chambers of the temple.

Hollywood would love this screenplay. If I were to cast Jehosheba in the movie, there are many Jewish actresses who would do an outstanding job. At the top of my list would be Academy Award-winning Jewish-American actress Natalie Portman. She has already played a compassionate Queen Padmé in *Star Wars: Episode III: Revenge of the Sith* and an anti-government revolutionary in *V for Vendetta*. A close second might be Israeli actresses Gal Gadot or Niv Sultan. (Watch the Apple TV+ series *Tehran*.)

In hindsight, what a great plan! Athaliah was no fan of Yahweh, and the worship of Yahweh and so he likely spent little time in the temple. The prince could be safe for a little while, at least.

But it took longer than they might have imagined. For seven years, the sole Davidic heir was kept hidden from royal spies. Finally, Jehoiada initiated a well-planned coup d'état, placing the rightful Davidic heir on the Judean throne and, to the cheers of the people, assassinating the usurper Queen. (2 Kings 11:4-18)

Unfortunately, we do not know what happened to Jehosheba. I assume she was greatly rewarded for her heroism and likely went on to live a normal life. Jo'ash began his reign at age 7 and served for 40 years.

I would love to tell you that Jo'ash reversed all the anti-Yahwistic policies of his grandmother and grandfather and was remembered for "walking with the Lord." It started quite positively. He initiated early reforms and the removal of much of the Baal worship in the land. But in his later years, he became one of the worst kings of Judah and abandoned the worship of Yahweh completely. He even had the prophet Zechariah stoned, and according to one source, he even claimed to be a god. He was assassinated by his own servants in 796 BCE. He was succeeded by his son, Amaziah, continuing the promised line of David.

Due to his wickedness and his turning away from God, Joash is one of only four Davidic kings <u>not</u> included in the genealogy of Jesus.

Though we are not specifically told, I think it is a matter of deductive reasoning to conclude God was *very* involved in this dangerous rescue scenario. I believe, like other heroes of Israel who were specifically called by God to vanquish a powerful enemy—think Deborah, Gideon, Samson, Elijah, and so many others—the Spirit of God also came upon Princess Jehosheba to accomplish her charge. Just look at the fingerprints.

Spirit-Sourced Fruit

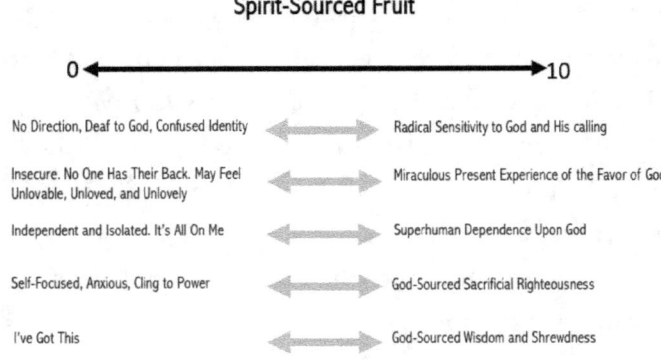

No Direction, Deaf to God, Confused Identity		Radical Sensitivity to God and His calling
Insecure. No One Has Their Back. May Feel Unlovable, Unloved, and Unlovely		Miraculous Present Experience of the Favor of God
Independent and Isolated. It's All On Me		Superhuman Dependence Upon God
Self-Focused, Anxious, Cling to Power		God-Sourced Sacrificial Righteousness
I've Got This		God-Sourced Wisdom and Shrewdness

In the moment, Jehosheba was willing to sacrifice her own life and put herself and her family in great danger to prevent a great violent injustice. She reflected what we refer to as "God-sourced sacrificial righteousness," one of the five fingerprints of empowerment by God's Spirit. Also, when I think of this account, I think of Zipporah, who just seemed to miraculously know what God wanted her to do, well before Moses did. Likewise, Jehosheba acted, it would seem, with great confidence. How much of God's plan was she aware of? You decide.

One way or another, I will say this. She and her actions are what God-sourced righteousness would look like fleshed out. Such righteousness motivates the person involved to put the safety and well-being of others over their own. You care for those who are hungry and needy and protect the vulnerable. You do the right thing, though it could cost you dearly. God-sourced righteousness (Hebrew: *tsaddiq*) is that Spirit-sourced biblical power and trait that empowers a person with superhuman concern for the well-being of others, even though they risk everything, including their own lives.

Jehosheba was a woman whose life was dramatically changed when I believe, she became filled with this Spirit-sourced righteousness. Jehosheba should have her own column in the Israelite Hall of Fame. She was a savior of Israel.

One last time, I want to encourage you again to keep saying the *Simple Uncluttered Gospel*[1] twice a day for 45 days. If you have been doing this, I would love to hear what you have been experiencing. Are you feeling more loveable, more loved, and even more lovely? Are you feeling that God has your back? More secure in your own skin, relationships, and calling? Do you get a little more of what child psychologist Urie Bronfenbrenner said about children?[2] "Every child needs at least one adult who is irrationally crazy about him or her." Are you feeling that God, Jesus, and the Spirit are irrationally crazy about you—as you are?

In the next chapter, I want to try to bring it all home. What can we learn from the amazing stories of these all-too-often overlooked and underappreciated women, true heroes of Israel and the church?

Engage Questions

1. What did you learn that you didn't know before?

2. Where did you resonate with Jehosheba?

3. What might Jehosheba want to tell you if you could speak to her right now?

---

1. You can get Simple Uncluttered Gospel bookmarks at https://gospel-app.com/product/women-simple-uncluttered-gospel-bookmarks /.

2. This irrational love is not a function of our success or record. We Jesus-followers understand that Jesus purchased this effectual assurance for us 2000 years ago. It is ours. But, after thirty plus years of ministry, I have observed that too many Christians, women, and men equally, struggle to experience this day to day. Many haven't felt it for a long time. This needs to change. The Spirit can make regular, shamed, doubt-riddled, failure-prone people like us grasp the limitless love of God for us as we are right now, not as we should be or could be. This is far better than anyone else has ever treated us. This is way beyond what we deserve. We can never get there through reason, apologetics, or even theology classes. We can't just 'choose' to feel it. Too good to believe? The Holy Spirit can change "If it is too good to believe, then it must not be true," to "It is too good to believe, but for some reason I actually believe and am beginning to experience it."

Chapter Nine

In Closing

T hough we are not specifically told, I believe the prime motivator for these amazing women was God's Spirit, who called and empowered them to do something that was beyond their capabilities, way beyond their training and experience. This is how God rolled in the Old Testament for women and men alike.

In some cases, we are specifically told.

In Exodus 35, God specifically chose the artist Bezalel "and filled him with the Spirit of God, with skill, ability, and knowledge in all kinds of crafts—to make artistic designs for work in gold, silver, and bronze" for the Tabernacle (Exodus 35:31-35).

In Numbers 11, God put the Spirit upon Moses' new seventy elders so they could co-lead the people in the wilderness. The sign of the transaction was that they prophesied (Num 11:25-26).

Some are specifically described as receiving the Spirit of God for some purpose. That illustrious list includes Joshua (Num 27:18, Dt 34:9), Balaam (Num 24:2), the Judges Othniel (Judges 3:10), Gideon (Judges 6:34), Jepthah (Judges 11:29), Samson (Judges 13:25, 14:6, 19), kings Saul (1 Sam 11:6), David (1Sam 16:13), Saul's army (1 Sam 19:20), the General Amasai (1 Chr 12:18), the prophets Elijah, Elisha, Azariah (2 Chr 15:1), Jehaziel (2 Chr 20:14), Zechariah (2 Chr 24:20), and so many others.

But even though the Bible doesn't specifically say so, I am sure this list should be expanded to include the Judge-Prophetess Deborah, the prophetesses Miriam (Ex 15:20), Huldah (2Chr 34:22) and Noadiah (Neh 6:14).

This is how God worked in the early days of Israel. In the New Testament, we understand all believers are filled with the Spirit (Eph 3:14-21). In the Old Testament, God often moves the narrative by choosing specific people and empowering them with specific gifts of the Spirit so they can accomplish their specific missions.

Spirit-Sourced Fruit

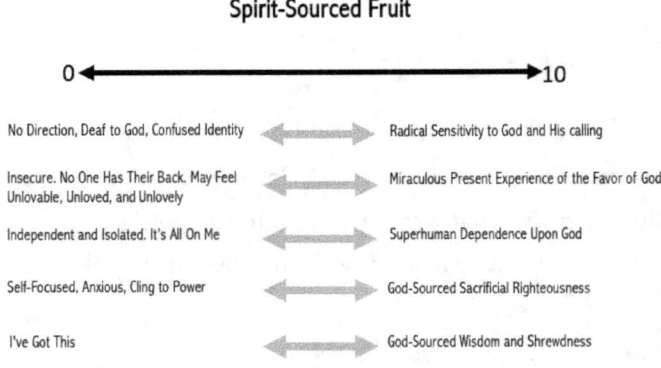

0 ⟵⟶ 10

No Direction, Deaf to God, Confused Identity	Radical Sensitivity to God and His calling
Insecure. No One Has Their Back. May Feel Unlovable, Unloved, and Unlovely	Miraculous Present Experience of the Favor of God
Independent and Isolated. It's All On Me	Superhuman Dependence Upon God
Self-Focused, Anxious, Cling to Power	God-Sourced Sacrificial Righteousness
I've Got This	God-Sourced Wisdom and Shrewdness

Looking at the *Spirit-Sourced Fruit* chart one more time, we can see some of the evidence of such Spirit empowerment. I believe all of these were observable in Eve and Adam pre-fall. In the cases of the remarkable women we met in this book, I think we can see such evidence.

A Radical Sensitivity to God and His Calling

Zlelponi, the mother of Samson, unlike her dull husband, just seemed to get that it was God speaking to her. The conversation didn't seem to make her anxious or fearful. I would be terrified. She calmly left the encounter, somehow confident of what needed to be done and *she* was the one to do it. When God found her, it would appear she was largely insecure and silenced by her context. Afterward, when we see her, she is an equal partner with her husband. She has been touched and honored by God, empowered by God's Spirit, and became a mother in Israel.

I am learning from her how much I need God to hear God. My tendency is just to try harder on my own. God raised up Zlelponi and empowered her to do what was needed to rescue Israel. Zlelponi didn't overthink it. She seemed to just enjoy the ride. In the end, she has become one of the twenty-three truly upright and righteous women who came forth from Israel.[1] God can do that.

Miraculous Present Experience of the Favor of God

Hannah seemed to believe she had fallen out of favor with her husband, and it drove her to despair. The taunting by wife #2, Beautiful Flowing Hair, didn't help matters. But she knew what *she* needed to do. She went to the Tabernacle of God in Shiloh and looked up into the *lipnay Elohim* (the face of God) so she might experience the miraculous favor of God toward her. She was granted that, along with her request for a son. She went into the intimate presence of God with a "bad heart," deeply troubled, filled with great anguish, and sad with vexation, unable to find emotional and relational relief or justice. When she left her encounter with God, we were told "her face was no longer to her," meaning her bad heart was miraculously renewed. I believe only the Spirit of God coming upon her can accomplish such a thing.

Superhuman Dependence on God

Hannah is also a good example of what can happen to a regular person who is going through periods of distress, inequities, injustices, and feelings of abandonment. She somehow knew her savior was not of flesh. Her husband could not fix the situation. Even if Beautiful Flowing Hair repented of her ugliness toward Hannah, the inequity remains. Hannah was infertile and desperately wanted a child. Her husband could stack her plate with all the meat he wanted, yet there was still nothing. Somehow, Hannah was singularly dependent on God to raise her up, speak into her emptiness, and raise up new life.

I have learned this from her. I tend to depend on so many things other than God to fix my problems. She was laser-focused on her trust and dependence on God and God's Spirit.

God-Sourced Sacrificial Righteousness

Princess Jehosheba didn't have to risk her life and well-being for the sake of an infant prince. She was married to the high priest. She had all of the benefits of being in the royal family. Plus, the odds were vastly stacked against her pulling this off. She was not Special Forces-trained. She did not have a crack team surrounding her. She was alone. And yet, something happened within her to make her step up and do what she could to rescue the crown prince. Sure, humans often sacrifice themselves for the sake of others. One doesn't need the power of the Spirit of God to do kind things, be hospitable, and treat others with honor and respect. To the extent we are thinking of others over ourselves, we are acting "God-like," to be sure.

Having said that, when someone like Jehosheba, me, or you is filled with God's Spirit, they will necessarily begin to think of others more than themselves, a little or a lot. It is one of the core fingerprints of God, Jesus, and the Spirit. Jehosheba was tossed into a situation where the promised line of David was at stake. Undoubtedly, the desire to risk all to save the crown prince was motivated by the Holy Spirit coming upon her.

I am learning from Jehosheba and from how God worked through regular people like her that the future just might be very interesting. If God could empower her with the Spirit, why not me? I am excited about that possibility—and a bit scared.

God-Sourced Wisdom and Shrewdness

Ya'el was likely a respected matriarch of her tribe. Left alone in the camp, going about her many responsibilities, she had little foreknowledge of what God was about to throw at her. Even if she was given a heads-up, what difference would that have made? General Sisera was no fool. There was no more greatly feared man in the region. He was a smart and capable warrior. She was no match for him. And remember, her people were on his side. There was a peace covenant. She needed not worry, unless...

Then God. Nowhere are we specifically told that God's Spirit came upon her, commanding her to ignore the peace treaty and all the cultural prescriptions surrounding hospitality. Nowhere are we told the exact instructions given to her. But we can deduce that she understood what she needed to do.

Here is what I am learning from Ya'el. God-sourced wisdom makes the recipient a little more aware of the ongoing, often invisible conflict between God and His enemies, the latter who seek to destroy God's people. These women and men seem willing to enter the fray, no matter the cost.

To defeat the enemy, they have been empowered with fantastic God-sourced wisdom, diplomacy, and rhetorical skills to usher shalom into contentious situations—at times without even a shot fired.

The Wise Woman of Abel-Beth-Maacha uses brilliant God-sourced diplomacy to make the feared General Joab stand down. She saves an entire city, including tens of thousands of God's people.

Sometimes, like Ya'el, bearers of God-sourced wisdom use disinformation, obfuscation, and even flat-out lies to protect the vulnerable people of God. But from God's point of view, there are times in the conflict with the enemy when strategy calls for misinformation. It is a war, and the potential costs are high. These women and men filled with God-sourced wisdom get it. In war, there is a place for subterfuge.

Ya'el deceives the powerful Canaanite General, offering him hospitality before she hammers a stake into his head. She is applauded for her effort by Judge Deborah and subsequent Jewish scholars. She should be honored with her own column in the Old Testament Hall of Women.

When God came to these amazing women, none of them were prepared for what God would ask of them. They were rightly afraid and skeptical, and they lacked confidence they were anywhere near the right person for such an auspicious calling.

From their largely patriarchal culture, they probably received explicit or implicit messaging that there were so many others—often men—who were better qualified, better equipped, better prepared, more righteous, more faithful, stronger, better leaders, better communicators, better resumes, and frankly, better overall choices than them. They likely had their own critical inner voices that condemned them regularly as well. That is all part of being human in this "groaning creation" (Rom 8:22). But then God...

"I want you to use your wisdom and your words to single-handedly convince one of the most arrogant, feared, and dangerous generals in the land to stop his siege of your city and to withdraw. I am using you to shame him. You and you alone will save your city."

"I know what my angel is asking of you. Trying to get pregnant has been a source of great shame and has caused your husband to think so little of you. I want you to trust me. Go get pregnant. Your son will begin the long-awaited salvation of Israel. This is on you. You can't make your husband be on board here."

"I want you to go against all the rules of hospitality you have ever known. You are forfeiting your reputation as a good host. Many will be shocked and critical of you for what I am asking you to do. The risks are higher than you can imagine. There is no other fit for this task. You must do this alone. I want you to lure the serial murderer of so many of my people into your tent, your bed, convince him you are as safe as his mother would be, and there kill him."

"I want you to step out of your cultural role and boundaries. Unless you do, your son will die. Do not assume your husband or others will do what needs to be done. Expect criticism for your overt actions. You will be accused of usurping authority. But hear me. I am the source of all authority, and I am giving it to you. I want you to step up to become a redeemer in Israel."

Many of these women were no doubt terrified of stepping up. The cost of falling down was overwhelming. They likely imagined what failure looked like and felt like in their contexts. What would cause them to leave their safe space and enter dangerous territory? What might their spouses or neighbors say of them? "Uppity, don't know their place, shameful, rebellious, a threat?" They could hear the ridicule now. "Who do you think you are? Are you better than me, than the men, than your husband? Get back in your place." But then God says, "You are the one I have chosen."

Gentle and Lowly

I am in debt to Dane C. Ortlund for his very important book, *Gentle and Lowly: The Heart of Christ for Sinners and Sufferers*[2]. The book should be read by every Christian—over and over again. It is very powerful. In one chapter,

Ortlund shares John Bunyan's (16th CT) unpacking of the verse where Jesus says, "Him that cometh to me I will in no wise cast out" (KJV). He is reflecting on men's and women's internal hesitancies about coming to Christ in the first place. Why would He come for me? He of all people has to know who I really am. I am unworthy. Track me here. You'll see where I head with this.

Bunyan writes:

> "They that are coming to Jesus Christ, are often times heartily afraid that Jesus Christ will not receive them. This observation is implied in the text. I gather it from the largeness and openness of the promise: "I will in no wise cast out." ...[But] this word, "in no wise," cuts the throat of all objections; and it was dropped by the Lord Jesus for that very end; and to help the faith that is mixed with unbelief. And it is, as it were, the sum of all promises; neither can any objection be made upon the unworthiness that you find in yourself, that this promise will not assoil."

With apologies to Ortlund and Bunyan, I want to adapt their thoughts regarding salvation and apply them to our hesitancies to hear and embrace sometimes dangerous callings from God.

So, you say,

"But I am not qualified; there are so many better prepared than me."

"I will be with you always," says Christ.

"But I am a flawed sinner; I am not a righteous, faithful, a good-enough woman or man."

"I will be with you always," says Christ.

"But I am too old and stuck in my ways."

"I will be with you always," says Christ.

"But I don't have the faith."

"I will be with you always," says Christ.

"But I am terrified."

"I will be with you always," says Christ.

"But no one will listen to me or to my voice."

        "I will be with you always," says Christ.

"But I have failed so many times before."

        "I will be with you always," says Christ.

"But I will be criticized, mocked, and become a trope for people who don't know their place. I will be made fun of."

        "I will be with you always," says Christ.

"But what if it is not really You who has spoken to me?"

        "I will be with you always," says Christ.

With apologies again to Dane Ortlund, I am absconding this quote of his referring specifically to our resistance to run to Jesus as our salvation. My alterations are noted.

"Fallen, anxious sinners [men and women alike] are limitless in their capacity to perceive reasons for Jesus [not to call them to a truly important task]. We are factories of fresh resistance to Christ's love. Even when we run out of tangible reasons to [demur], such as specific sins or failures, we tend to retain a vague sense that, given enough time, Jesus will finally grow tired of us and [stop having our backs]. Bunyan understands us. He knows we tend to deflect Christ's assurances."

Bunyan again (my alterations noted).

"No, wait"—you say, cautiously approaching Jesus—"you don't understand. I've messed up in all kinds of ways."

        "I know," He responds.

"But I don't know if I can break free of this any time soon."

        "That's the only kind of person I'm here to help."

"The burden is heavy—and heavier all the time."

        "Then let me carry it."

"It's too much to bear."

        "Not for me."

"You don't get it. [My lack of faith is not just in my capability. I lack faith in You. I don't believe you love me that much, as I am.]"

"[Then I am the one most suited to give you fresh heaven-sourced faith so you will begin to experience my love for you. My love loves the unlovable, the unloved, and the unlovely. It is my love for the unworthy that begins to make them truly worthy]."

Readers, I hope to encourage us to begin to see some of the amazing possibilities being laid before us by Jesus, before you in particular, as you are, not as you should be or could be. No matter what you've done or not done in the past, no matter what you've said or not said, no matter whether you are educated enough, attractive enough, smart enough, wise enough, faithful enough, liked enough, or anything *enough*. Whether you feel ready or not, you have no idea just how unique and special you are. This world just beats the significance and worth out of you. No judgment.

Follow my logic here. There must be a compelling reason why you and I are still on "terra firma" and not fully enjoying the endless riches and vast wholeness of heaven. If God loves you so much that He sent His only beloved Son to cruelly perish so you would enjoy a relationship with Him beyond description, then why wouldn't He immediately open the doors of heaven so that you, right now, would experience the utter fullness of the height, width, length, and depth of the love of Christ for you?

But if you are reading this, you are still being restrained, abused, and violated by this present evil age to one degree or another. This is true for each one of us, a little or a lot.

The only conclusion I can possibly come to is that God is not finished with you and me here. There must be a task, calling, or mission only you can do. Make sense? If someone else could do it, you would be immediately grabbed to enter the celestial dance of the Trinity. Jesus purchased that for you 2000 years ago. You have nothing more to prove or to earn.

I am not proposing you drop everything and do something dramatic on your own. God is more than capable of making you know what He has for you.

My suggestion is you keep saying the *Simple Uncluttered Gospel*³ twice a day. After you vocalize it, hold your empty hands up skyward and just be quiet and listen. God, why am I here? What can I do? Make me know that you have my back.

Here it is, one more time. Let the words wash over you. Just breathe and drink it in. Ask the Spirit to come upon you, like Zipporah, Zlelponi, Jehosheba, Ya'el, the Wise Women of Abel-Beth-Maacha, and Hannah.

> Jesus-Follower, strictly because of what Jesus did for you 2000 years ago, Jesus loves you with all His heart, as much as the Father loves the Son and the Son loves the Father. He loves you as you are, not as you should be or could be. You can't add to this love or take away from it. It often feels like you've messed it up or need to do something so God will like you better. Not so. How do you experience it more? Simple! Ask the Spirit inside of you to make you know, experience, and feel just how much God loves you right now. Just ask. Ask again later today. Ask tomorrow. Make it a spiritual habit.

What do you think?

I suspect if you are like me, you may be hesitant. I get it. Is this dangerous? Yep. Could this be messy? Yep, usually. Could you get it wrong? I do all the time. What if Jesus has abandoned you? Or is He disappointed in you for not hearing him in the past, or did you just bullheadedly do your own thing because you thought it was right? You will mess up—a little or a lot. Yet He adores you always the same, as much as the Father loves the Son and the Spirit, and the Son and the Spirit love the Father. You cannot mess that up. He can't be any more proud of you than He is right now. Jesus purchased that for you as well. You are playing with 'bank money.'

———⊰❈⊱———

In the next *Dance, Daughters of the Most High* Volume, we will look at more amazing Old Testament women who have unfortunately been overlooked, underappreciated, or just plain misunderstood. For the most part, like you, they were just regular, real women living their real lives in this real world. They had not planned on being tapped by God for special service, which is often very dangerous. But then God...

See you then! Take heart, daughters and sons of God.

I love to hear feedback from you. What struck you? Do you have stories that would encourage others? Please share them with me. And if you want to know when the next *Dance, Daughter of the Most High (Volume 2)* will be published, write me an email at Bill@Gospel-App.com. Also, check out my weekly podcast, *Gospel Rant.*

---

1. In Kadari, "Wife of Manoach."

2. Ortlund, " *Gentle and Lowly.* "

3. You can get Simple Uncluttered Gospel bookmarks at https://gospel-app.com/product/women-simple-uncluttered-gospel-bookmarks /.

www.ingramcontent.com/pod-product-compliance
Lightning Source LLC
Chambersburg PA
CBHW060541130626
46553CB00002B/845